THE
CONTEMPORARY CRAFT
OF PAPER MACHE

THE
CONTEMPORARY CRAFT
OF PAPER MACHE

Techniques ▪ Projects ▪ Inspirations

Helga Meyer

Photography by Hayo Heye

Lark Books

Illustrations: Helga Meyer, Hamburg, Germany
Layout: Helga Meyer and Birgit Blohmann Studio, Basel, Switzerland
Production: Celia Naranjo
Translation from the German: Mary Killough

Library of Congress Cataloging-in-Publication Data
Meyer, Helga
    [Papiermache. English]
    The contemporary craft of paper mache : techniques, projects,
inspirations / Helga Meyer ; photography by Hayo Heye.
             p. cm.
    Translation of: Papiermache.
    Includes bibliographical references and index.
    ISBN 1-887374-11-6
    1. Papier-mâché. I. Title.
  TT871.M4813 1996
745.54'2—dc20
                                    96-22299
                                      CIP

10 9 8 7 6 5 4 3 2 1

Published by Lark Books, 50 College St., Asheville, NC 28801

Originally published as Helga Meyer, *Papiermache: Ideen und Techniken fur kreatives Gestalten*,
 Verlag Paul Haupt (Bern, Stuttgart, Wien), 1996.

Distributed in the U.S. by Sterling Publishing, 387 Park Ave. South, New York, NY 10016; 800/367-9692
Distributed in Canada by Sterling Publishing,
 c/o Canadian Manda Group, One Atlantic Ave., Suite 105, Toronto,
 Ontario, Canada M6K 3E7

Printed in Italy

ISBN 1-887374-11-6

CONTENTS

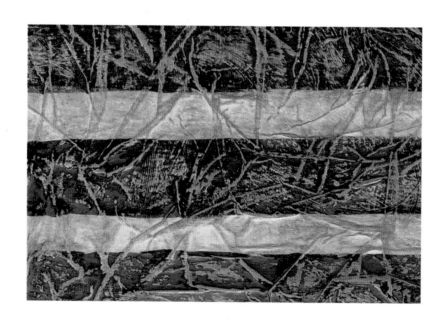

FOREWORD

Paper was always one of my favorite materials, because of its versatility. And paper mache? I don't know when, but at some time it entered my consciousness and then slowly conquered it completely.

For me it began—how else?—with pasting paper on a balloon. That first balloon bowl stood on my window sill until I finally found it too simple and attacked it with scissors. What ultimately emerged was the blue bowl with the segmented rim on page 32.

After a few more balloon bowls from layered paper (and also from paper mache pulp), I began to long for more variety. I thought about getting away from the old predictable forms, and I began to look at all objects and wonder whether they could be reproduced in paper mache. In time, I was able to create the most varied objects from this versatile material.

This book begins with a chapter that explains the basic techniques and procedures, so that they do not need to be repeated for each individual project. The next eight chapters introduce paper mache objects for a variety of uses. The final chapter deals with the broad field of surface decoration.

The first few objects introduced can be created with the simplest materials; from them you can learn the basic techniques. In the chapters that follow, you will find still more simple projects, but also more elaborate objects and an introduction to special methods of work.

While the description of each project explains how it was created, my intention is not merely to tell you how to copy the object exactly. Rather, the instructions are intended to inform and stimulate your own interpretations and designs.

I put great value on experimentation and would like to encourage you, the reader, to do that as well. On the other hand, I do not want to abandon you with that directive, but rather to put as much of my experience at your service as possible.

As for the creation of this book, I wish to thank photographer Hayo Heye, who captured my paper mache objects in many beautiful photographs with great interest and care. Thank you for your outstanding assistance!

In addition, I wish to thank my husband, who for years has submitted in silence to paper mache as a topic of conversation and endured it when I laid siege to the kitchen with bags full of paper scraps, buckets, and bowls, and covered everything with spatterings of paper pulp. During the final weeks of work on this book, he made sure I did not starve, read the proofs, and created the index.

Meanwhile, even my cat has developed a taste for little bits of paper. She enthusiastically fashions—well, tears—every cardboard carton she can get hold of into small bite-sized pieces, which she then spreads evenly and artistically over the floor.

1

Techniques for Paper Mache Materials, Tools, and Instructions

In this chapter, the necessary materials and tools for producing paper mache will be described, and the working methods for the layering technique and paper mache from pulp will be thoroughly explained. This information will serve as the basis for making objects that will be introduced in the following chapters.

- *What is Paper Mache?*

- *Materials and Tools for the Layering Technique*

- *Paper for Layering*

- *Materials and Tools for Paper Mache From Pulp*

- *Preparing the Pulp*

- *Recipes for Pulp*

- *Working With Pulp*

- *Forms I, II, and III*

- *Assembling the Parts*

What Is Paper Mache?

Paper mache is a material that consists of paper and binder. It can be created in two ways.

The first method gave the material its name: the term *paper mache* means "chewed paper" (French *macher* means "to chew"). Preparing the material and working with it occur in two steps. First paper is cut into small pieces and mixed with water and a binder into a mass of fiber called *pulp*. Then it is shaped in a manner similar to modelling clay.

In the second method, the material and the object are created simultaneously, in one process. The paper is pasted together in many layers, one on top of the other, so that a stable shell of paper is created. Fixing many layers of paper together is called *the layering technique* or *layering*.

Objects made from pulp paper mache are essentially different from those made of layered paper mache. Pulp objects are thick and appear heavier compared to the lightness and thinness of layered pieces. In appearance, the thin walls of layered objects resemble somewhat the fragility of eggshells, but layered pieces are astonishingly strong. In the process of drying, their surface becomes slightly wavy or creased. The characteristic of the material is somewhere between that of textiles and wood. Pulp paper mache is very compact but is nevertheless a relatively loosely structured and light material. After the moisture between the fibers of the pulp dries out, a typically fine-grained structure results.

Materials and Tools for Layered Paper Mache

The process of creating paper objects from paper glued together in layers is easy to follow, and it requires a minimum of materials and tools. The basic supplies are rather simple: paper, paste, a paintbrush, lubricant, and a form—that is, something on which to paste the strips of paper. (More about suitable forms on page 23). There is no preparatory work, and only a small amount of paper is needed; however, a certain amount of patience is required. The drying process is quite a bit shorter than with paper mache from pulp, so that once begun, work on objects can be continued much more quickly. Layering is well suited for the beginner.

Tools

The only tool needed for the layering technique is a flat paintbrush, which is used for both pasting the paper scraps together and pressing them firmly onto the object you are making. The width of the brush depends on the size of the object; for very large surfaces, a wide paintbrush is suitable.

A sharp craft knife, heavy scissors, a compass, and a pencil are needed for working with the layered paper shell. More about this under "assembly."

Lubricants

In order to keep the paper layers from sticking to the form, it is usually necessary to apply a lubricant to the form. Petroleum jelly or a simple hand cream can be used; soft soap also works. For very intricate forms—plaster molds, for example—it is advisable to use a small bristle brush. You must proceed very carefully; otherwise, problems may arise when removing the form from the finished paper mache. Unfortunately, lubricants tend to be slightly greasy—which is annoying when the grease appears on visible parts.

An alternative to using lubricants is to dip the first two layers of paper into water, place these on the form, and press them onto the form with a clean paintbrush until they are firmly secured. Then start using paste beginning with the third layer. A third option is to wrap the form with plastic or aluminum wrap.

Adhesives

The adhesive holds the paper layers together. Together, these two materials form the working material, paper mache. The adhesive creates the great strength.

Wallpaper Paste

Wallpaper paste is the best adhesive for layered paper mache. There are several varieties: normal cellulose paste, and special paste with synthetic resin binder added.

It is best to use a glass jar with a rust-proof lid for stirring the paste. It is sufficient to begin with a small amount—enough for one or two days' work. The paste should be quite thick: approximately two level tablespoons of powder sprinkled into a pint (half a liter) of water and stirred immediately. The paste must be mixed for 20 minutes—stirred and shaken vigorously—so that it does not form lumps or deposits. If paste stands too long, it loses its adhesive power; when that happens, it becomes watery.

Flour Paste

Flour paste is a good alternative for people allergic to commercial paste and for children, too. Add two level tablespoons of flour (about 15 grams) to one-half cup (1 dl) water in a glass jar. With the lid on, shake the jar vigorously until no lumps of flour remain. Pour the mixture into a saucepan, add a little less than two-thirds cup of water (1.50 dl), and let it simmer over low heat, stirring constantly until it is thick.

PVA Wood Glue

Available at every craft shop, hardware store, and discount mart, this glue goes by many names: white glue, craft glue, and (its real name) polyvinyl acetate, or PVA. It is also available in a somewhat stronger and quicker-drying formula, sold primarily to woodworkers and known as wood glue.

PVA wood glue is a very stable and versatile adhesive made of synthetic resin. It can be diluted with water. You can add it to paste to increase its adhesive power when pasting thicker types of paper. It is somewhat unpleasant to use, as it sticks to your hands very readily.

Undiluted wood glue is good for assembling paper objects. It is also a good binder for pigments and similar materials.

In the remaining pages, PVA glue will be called simply "wood glue."

Paper for Layering

In general, the highest-quality paper will give you the best results. In addition, it is best to choose paper that can be worked with easily. Based on my experience, I prefer thin paper, especially tissue paper. While you will reach the desired strength more quickly with heavy paper, it also has many disadvantages.

■ *Tissue Paper*

Tissue paper combined with paste results in very firm paper mache. It is pleasant to work with, because it adheres very nicely to the form and sticks together well. It can be worked quickly, because you can use larger scraps than you can of heavier paper. Any creases that arise can be smoothed away easily. You do not need to soften it to make it flexible after pasting it. On the contrary, you need to work with it immediately or it can easily become highly breakable.

Tissue paper comes in various qualities and thicknesses. The best type is the somewhat stronger kind that cannot be torn easily; it is widely used as wrapping paper for flowers. Since layering does not require large amounts of paper, you can easily collect what you need. You can buy this tissue paper by the roll at a reasonable price from a store that sells florist supplies. This paper has one smooth, slightly glossy side, which often has print on it, and a matte underside. Most layered objects in this book are made from this paper. For outside surfaces, you should use white, unprinted paper, so that you have a neutral background on which to create decorated surfaces.

In addition, there are various grey tissue papers that are used as packing material or for padding furniture. Many of those are very suitable; others are not, because they are too brittle or too inflexible. Normally, types with both a dull side and a glossy side can easily be used. It is wise to experiment with any paper before committing yourself to a major project.

Stationery stores carry especially fine tissue paper, packaged in sheets and available in many colors. This paper is much too thin for the layering technique; it is difficult to use because it tears easily. In addition, the colored varieties lose their color when wet.

■ *Newsprint*

Newsprint is often recommended for paper mache, probably because it is available in great quantity and because people find it is easy to get. But these advantages are balanced by the fact that this heavier paper takes longer to work with. You have to tear it into smaller pieces, because it is less pliant and creases more readily. It absorbs a lot of moisture, so that both sides of it must be coated with paste, and it is necessary to let the paste soak in for a while so that the paper becomes flexible.

Newsprint is of lesser quality and therefore results in a paper shell that is not as firm. For added strength, you can add wood glue to the paste.

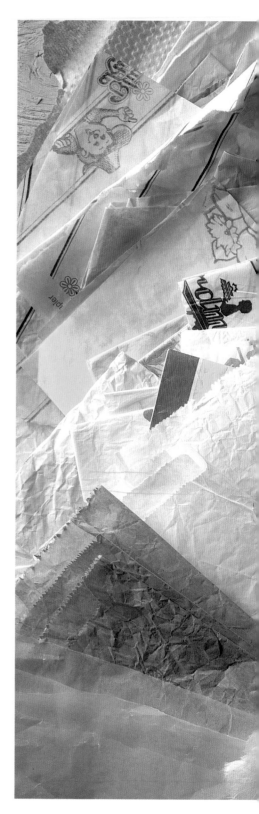

Kite Paper

Available in craft and hobby stores in individual sheets, kite paper is a very high-quality, firm, tough, transparent paper. Often used for making Christmas lanterns, window hangings, and (of course) kites, it also forms a very durable layer of paper mache. It stretches a great deal when wet and shrinks even more when it dries. You can use it for the entire project or for the outermost layer only.

Because it is transparent, it is especially suitable for lamps or other fragile objects, where the paper layers need to be thin enough for light to shine through. Three to four layers form a membrane similar to parchment—somewhat creased and irregularly transparent.

If you paste kite paper to the outside of a firm paper shell, you can stretch it to create a very smooth and resilient surface. If you paste one layer of kite paper over another, you can create interesting color effects. Always place the lighter shade on top of the darker one. Unfortunately, some of the colors tend to fade.

Packing Paper

Thin types of packing paper are well suited for layering, as long as they become pliable when wet. On the other hand, heavier packing paper is not appropriate, because it is too inflexible. In addition, some types are moisture proof and thus unworkable.

Ingres Paper

Ingres paper is a high-quality drawing paper. Available in many beautiful colors, it usually has an ingrained pattern of lines. As to its usefulness for layering, it is a borderline case, because it is actually somewhat too heavy and inflexible. But since there are scarcely any better alternatives in permanently colored paper, it is worth the effort to use this paper in exceptional cases. It must be torn into small pieces, coated heavily with paste, and thoroughly softened.

Rice Paper

The fiber structure of rice paper (also known as Japan paper) is very lovely. Since it is a costly material, you will want to limit its use to surfaces only. The effect is especially beautiful when you paste white Japan paper onto a darker background.

Unsuitable Paper

Some paper simply doesn't work well for layering. Included are paper that is too heavy and therefore too inflexible (typing paper, drawing paper, heavy packing paper, and handmade paper, for example); paper that is too soft (facial tissues, paper towels, and napkins); and paper whose color fades (dyed tissue paper and crepe paper, among others).

Layering on a Balloon

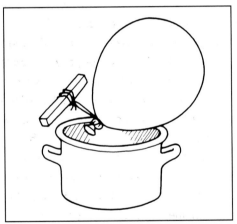

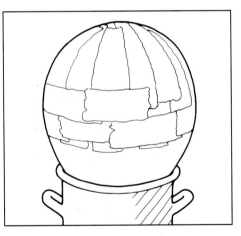

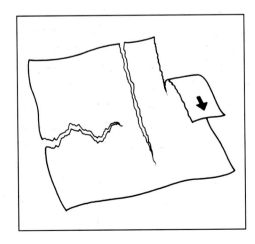

Layering on a balloon makes an ideal first project; it is very easy to do.

Before beginning to work, mix the paste and cover your work area with a large, flattened plastic bag, to protect the surface.

Blow up the balloon and knot it. Tie a weight to the knot and place it in a pot. Since the balloon will be punctured later, no lubricant is necessary.

Now tear a small amount of the paper into strips. Make a trial tear to find the direction of the grain of the paper. If you tear with the grain, you will be able to tear straight strips. The narrower the strips are, the better they can be shaped onto the round contours of the balloon without causing creases. Never cut the paper. Cut edges remain visible and have a tendency to come loose. By contrast, torn paper is fibrous on the edges, and the fibers adhere easily and without visible seams.

Now you can begin to apply the paper to the balloon. The first two layers and the last layer should be white tissue paper. They form the neutral background on which to apply paint later.

To begin, lay several strips of paper on the plastic bag and spread them with paste. Use quick motions when working with tissue paper, or it will tear apart easily. Place all the strips onto the balloon in the same direction, overlapping on both sides, and press them down firmly with the paintbrush. Air bubbles need to be carefully pressed out.

Layering on a Firm Object

Then paste the next layer to the balloon in the opposite direction—that is, one layer should lie perpendicular to the midpoint and the next layer horizontally around the balloon. This way, you can be sure that the entire surface is covered.

For the inside layers you can use printed tissue paper. It helps to alternate layers of different colored paper, because then you can see better how much of the surface is covered. Apply at least 15 layers of tissue paper, alternating directions. Again, the last two layers should be white.

If you want to use newsprint for the inside layers, you will need to paste it on both sides. It goes more quickly if you spread a thick coat of paste on the plastic bag, lay as many scraps of newsprint as possible on it, and then apply paste on the other side of the paper strips. Newsprint must be thoroughly covered with paste before you can work with it. Ten to 12 layers will be sufficient.

When the layers are complete, place the balloon in a warm place to dry—for example, on a heat vent. After it is dry, test to see if the paper is firm. If the paper shell "gives" when you press it, you may strengthen it with a few more layers.

When the paper shell is finished, puncture the balloon and remove it. The edge of the resulting shell can be cut away or remain irregular. Since a balloon shrinks during drying, the paper covering also contracts, forming a pattern of small folds.

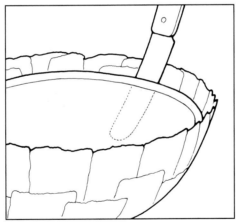

If you wish to paste paper strips onto a firm object, then you must consider several additional aspects, because the form will not be destroyed but will be removed in one piece from under the paper shell.

Cover the form with a lubricant so that the paper shell does not stick to it. When pressing the first layer of paper onto the form with the paintbrush, be careful not to brush over the lubricant, or it will get smeared. From then on, proceed exactly as you did with the balloon. To cover curved details without causing creases, use very small scraps of paper.

The relative ease of removing the form from the finished shell of paper depends on its shape. Open forms like bowls can be removed in one piece. If you have done your layering on the inside of a bowl, the paper layer comes off automatically, because it shrinks when drying. If layers are added to the outside, you should proceed carefully, using a flexible knife blade between the bowl and the paper shell to loosen it. Then pull the two apart—slowly.

For forms that are either tapered or completely covered by paper, the paper shell must be cut. For bottles, one long cut is usually enough. In most cases, you should cut the paper shell into two equal halves. If there are details such as handles, spouts, or feet, they must be cut through the middle axis.

The pieces must be put together again and the seams covered with paper strips. See the section on assembly.

Materials and Tools for Pulp

Working with paper mache from pulp is more time-consuming than layering at first, because the pulp must be prepared before you can begin working on the object you're creating. On the other hand, the actual work goes more quickly, because you use it like modelling clay. That is its advantage.

Implements and Tools

For preparing the pulp, you will need a bucket, several plastic bowls, possibly a large old cooking pot, a sieve, and a heavy kitchen hand towel. In addition, a food processor is absolutely essential for breaking down the wet paper.

A paper cutter is helpful for cutting up the paper. Even better is a paper shredder (also known as a document shredder), but these aids are not entirely necessary.

Although the pulp is worked primarily by hand, tools such as kitchen knives are useful for smoothing and modelling it. The workplace must be near running water and should be easy to clean.

Adhesives

Wallpaper paste is the ideal binder for pulp, as it is for layered paper mache. The powdered paste can be kneaded while dry into the paper pulp or stirred in to a very thick consistency. Further details will be given in the section about the preparation of pulp. Adding some wood glue to the pulp will increase its strength. (If you bound the pulp entirely with wood glue,

most of the adhesive would end up on your hands.) You can cover a finished object made from pulp with thinned wood glue in order to harden its surface.

In old recipes, bone glue is mentioned as the binder for pulp. Because soaking and heating bone glue is complicated and time-consuming, it is not very common anymore.

Lubricants

The earlier suggestions for lubricants and layering apply here as well, although lubricants do not have as pronounced an effect on pulp as on layered objects. Contrary to some sources, it is not advisable to use wet paper layers to separate the form and the pulp, because these layers cannot be separated from the pulp later.

Paper

The appearance and strength of the pulp will vary with the type of paper used. High-quality paper yields a firm material that can be polished or chiseled like wood. Poor-quality papers are essentially softer and can become brittle when they are worked on.

When dry, pulp paper mache has an interesting, rough surface texture, which does not necessarily require additional decoration. For that reason, a charming effect can result from using colored paper or even a variety of colors. The finished pa-

per mache will have approximately the same color as the original pulp. When choosing paper, color and quality are more important than strength.

Typing Paper

All paper for typewriters, computers, and photocopiers, as well as writing tablets, are very suitable. The whitest result is from heavily bleached copier paper (1). Used paper—that is, paper with printing or writing on it—can be added without hesitation. The particles of color add charming speckles (2). Even green-striped computer paper looks attractive (3). Use grey recycled paper only if you will be covering the object with paint later, because its color is not very appealing (4). White copier paper with sawdust added is also interesting (8).

Nowadays, document shredders are used in so many large offices that you can surely find someone who will supply you with shredded typing paper. That saves a lot of work.

Kitchen Paper and Facial Tissues

Paper towels (6) and facial tissues (7) are well suited for pulp paper mache. They result in a lovely, rather fine-grained material. The color fluctuates between pure white and a more natural-looking off-white.

◼ *Napkins*

Napkins produce a fine-textured material as well (5). In addition, colored napkins can easily be converted into colored paper mache. You can use them without adding any other paper (9,10), mix them together (11, 12), or lighten them with some white pulp (13, 14).

◼ *Colored Paper*

Other kinds of dyed paper, such as tinted paper (18) and colored photocopy paper (19), can be used for colored pulp. It is possible to mix them together or with other papers to create new colors.

◼ *Colored Handmade Paper*

This is an especially high-quality (and not exactly inexpensive) artist's paper, which is available in especially lovely nuances of colors. You can use it without adding any other paper (15, 17). For larger projects, two or three sheets in strong colors would be sufficient to color white pulp made from typing paper (16).

◼ *Not Recommended*

There are many types of lower-quality paper that are not recommended. Among them are packing paper (20), newspapers (21), magazine paper (22), and egg cartons (23). Entirely unsuitable are waterproof paper, such as packing paper, and types that fade, such as crepe paper and colored tissue paper.

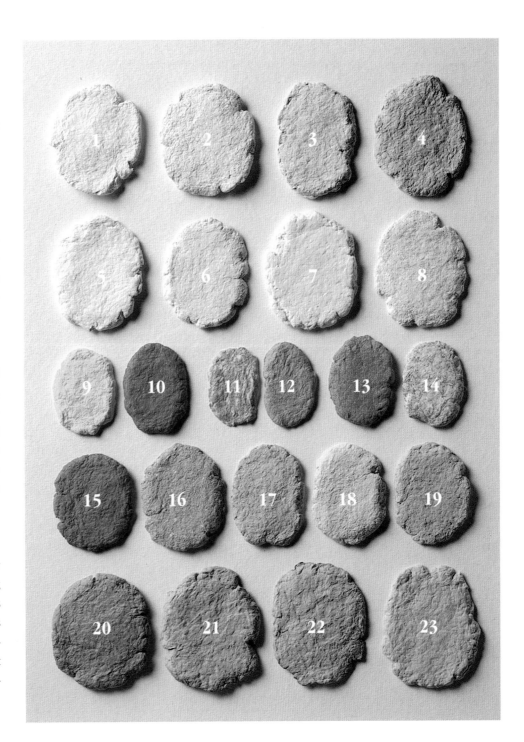

Preparing the Pulp

Much more paper is needed for pulp paper mache than for layered paper mache. Tear or cut the paper into pieces about one inch (2.5 cm) long. As a rule, the firmer the paper, the smaller the scraps must be. A paper cutter makes the work easier, but of course the easiest to use is shredded paper from an office. Don't worry if you don't have access to either of these aids: working by hand produces no lesser a product.

Soak the torn paper several hours in water. If necessary, you can speed the process of dissolving the paper by cooking it in a large pot, but, in my experience, this is not entirely advisable. If you rub the scraps that have been soaked vigorously between your hands, you will see the paper dissolve into fibers.

If you are using shredded paper, the long strips must be torn into short pieces so that they do not get caught in the blade of the food processor. Soaking the paper first makes the process much easier than using the material dry.

As the final step, "puree" the soaked paper in the food processor until it is in very small pieces. Add a portion at a time to the bucket and mix in a large amount of the water. Keep processing the material until there are no more paper fibers visible in the pulp. Then pour the pulp through a very fine mesh sieve.

Now place the mixture in a heavy kitchen hand towel and wring it out as vigorously as possible. This results in bizarre-looking balls of fiber.

After all the mixture is in balls of fiber, break them into pieces and place them in a large plastic bowl. Now add the paste. Use very thick paste so that very little additional water gets into the pulp. This mixture must be worked very carefully. Knead balls of it the size of your fist, a portion at a time; the longer you knead, the more workable the mixture.

If the mixture is too firm, add more paste to make it more workable. However, if it feels wet but not workable, press more moisture out and add more powdered paste. The paste powder has to be very thoroughly mixed in and kneaded so that there are no lumps. It will slowly soak up moisture and bind to the paper.

In order for the entire mass to attain the same consistency, press the balls flat and stack them in layers. Divide the piles into several "slices of cake" and knead those again. Now the pulp should be ready to work.

If you want colored paper mache, mixing paper of various colors can produce delightful results. There are two possibilities. If you put both colors—for example, white and blue—together in the food processor, they will turn out light blue. If you mix the colors together as you are kneading the mixture, you will get a blue and white speckled effect similar to granite.

To keep the pulp, wrap it in aluminum foil and store it in the refrigerator. However, it will only last a week at most. If the pulp is no longer workable but on the watery side, the paste has lost its adhesive quality. If necessary, you can salvage pulp in this condition by dissolving it in water, pressing the water out of it in a cloth, and adding new paste.

It is better to let the pulp dry if you are not going to work with it immediately. Later it can be moistened again and worked with paste.

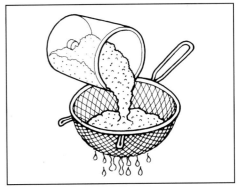

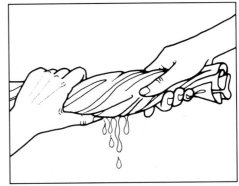

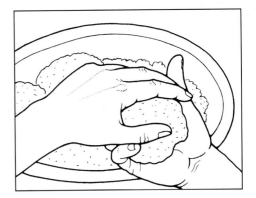

Recipes for Pulp

■ Basic Recipe for Pulp

About 10 ounces (300 g) dry paper

5 level tablespoons (30 g) powdered
wallpaper paste

About 4 cups (900 g) total water—in
the paper fibers and in the paste

Total weight of the pulp: about 2³/₄
pounds (1230 g)

■ Paper Mache With Sawdust

About 10 ounces (300 g) dry paper

3¹/₂ ounces (100 g) sifted sawdust

5 level tablespoons (30 g) powdered
wallpaper paste

3 tablespoons (30 ml) wood glue

About 5¹/₃ cups total water—in the paper fibers and in the paste

Total weight of the pulp: about 3
pounds 10 ounces (1660 g)

■ Paper Mache with Flour

About 10 ounces (300 g) dry paper

10 ounces (300 g) flour

5 level tablespoons powdered wallpaper paste

About 5¹/₃ cups (1200 g) total water—
in the paper fibers and in the paste

Total weight of the pulp: about 4
pounds (1830 g)

Note: These recipes are general guide-
lines, not scientific prescriptions. You will
have to decide for yourself when the pulp
has a workable consistency. It may help to
measure out the water first and use it to
mix with both the paper and the paste.

■ Additives

In historical recipes you will find the
most varied ingredients added to the pulp.
These recipes were developed for commercial mass production for use with plaster molds. Crayon, clay, charcoal ashes,
sawdust, flour, heavy spar, ground soap-
stone, and so on were used to stretch the
amount of paper in order to lower the
costs and make the consistency better.
Such additives made up more than 50 per-
cent of the pulp in many old recipes! The
mineral content made the paper finer, but
unfortunately it also made it heavier. It lost
its organic, wood-like character and was
harder to mold and cut.

I find organic material such as fine
sawdust and flour more suitable, because
they are more similar to the basic material—paper. But as a rule the more filler that
is added, the more the nature of the paper
is adulterated.

Some old recipes specify additives
such as tobacco juice, garlic, wormwood,
wintergreen oil, carnation oil, and so on.
They were used to retard spoilage and
mold. The usual wallpaper paste of today
already has preservatives and fungicide
added so that these complicated ingredients are not necessary.

Two of the recipes given here include
sawdust or flour as additives. Flour serves
to extend the material and refine its consistency; it makes pulp from white paper a
little yellowish. Flour pulp is very suitable
for use with plaster forms. Flour is very
sticky at first when you knead it; that less-
ens after the dough has rested a while.
Fine sawdust that has been sifted gives the
paper mache a brown speckled appearance (pattern number 8 on page 17).

Make sure that the added material har-
monizes with the color of the paper being
used.

■ Pulp from Paper Bags

Craft and hobby shops sell pulverized
(instant) paper mache. This material relates to homemade pulp about like instant
soup from a package relates to homemade
stew. I have nothing against this material
except that it looks uninteresting. Instant
paper mache has a very fine consistency
and often a light beige color, and it is certainly suitable for clown heads. But for the
discerning, aesthetically trained eye, it offers little inspiration.

Nevertheless, I work often and happily
with this material. Instead of mixing it with
water, I mix it with paste and use it as a
kind of putty to fill in uneven spots or to
make small corrections. Equally good for
this purpose is paper mache powder from
an artists' supply shop. Both materials create a smooth, firm surface. When finishing
the object, you must cover the putty with
paper or with a primer to make it invisible.

Working with Pulp

■ **Processing**

Before beginning work, you should always save a little of the prepared pulp in the refrigerator for possible corrections later.

When working on solid forms, you must first apply a layer of lubricant. On the other hand, rubber balls or flexible cardboard forms covered with foil can be separated easily without using a lubricant.

After the form is prepared, begin covering it with pulp. Distribute the pulp bit by bit onto the surface of the form until the form is covered entirely. Try to make the layer of pulp equally thick all over. Then press the pulp carefully onto the form, using your hands to create a covering without any gaps.

An alternative approach works well with very flat dishes or cylindrical forms. First place the pulp between two sheets of plastic wrap and use a rolling pin to roll the pulp into a flat mass. Remove the top sheet of plastic wrap, then wrap the flat pulp and the remaining plastic sheet around the outer surface of the form. Or lay the dish on the flat pulp, pick up a corner of the plastic wrap and the pulp, and roll the dish and the pulp up together. After you remove the second piece of plastic wrap, press the seam closed if necessary and smooth over the edges.

To finish, brush another coat of paste or water-thinned wood glue onto the surface of the pulp and smooth it out with a knife blade. The back of a spoon works better for interior surfaces. A small kitchen knife is an ideal tool for modelling the fine details and clean edges, and a little paste helps make the material more workable. After the surface of the pulp has dried out a bit, you can smooth out the curves again with a knife.

■ **Areas of Application**

It is true that paper mache pulp is a type of modelling material, but it would be wrong to compare it too closely with clay. Clay can be worked free-standing, while pulp—like layered paper mache—is modelled on a form. It forms a thick wall, approximately $1/8$ to a $1/4$ inch thick ($1/4$ to $1/2$ cm). Since pulp consists of coarser particles than clay, you cannot expect to be able to create details as precisely as in clay.

Forms such as tin cans, plastic containers, paper cups, and so on can be covered with pulp and then decorated with details also made of pulp. That is, in fact, the easiest way of working with this material. Flexible forms such as rubber balls and cardboard constructions can also serve as forms and are easily removed afterwards.

If you want to model on firm objects, you must consider the fact that dried pulp is not flexible and is thus more difficult to separate from the form than is layered paper mache. Therefore you should limit your pulp work to the inside of simple, open forms such as bowls.

Pulp is very useful for making copies of plaster molds. The technique allows for results with clean details.

The most varied decorative elements can be made of pulp to add to available basic forms. They are either modelled directly onto the shell of paper mache or finished separately and glued on with wood glue after they are dry.

■ **Drying**

The drying process for pulp paper mache takes a very long time, and the material shrinks in the process. Points of stress can result because the material dries faster at the edges than in the middle. It is advisable to keep an eye on the drying process in case it is necessary to place weights on certain places.

You can make corrections on dried pieces with a sharp knife and smooth them over with emery paper. You can correct small mistakes with the reserved pulp.

If you have used high-quality paper, you can leave the material as it is. You can change the color with transparent glazes without covering up the lovely surface with a coat of paint. If the paper mache is not so attractive, because it was made from scrap paper for example, you can decorate it in many different ways.

FORM I
Everyday Objects to Model

This section covers working with layered paper mache as well as with paper mache from pulp. It defines some terms you will find later and introduces the various kinds of forms—everyday objects, homemade forms, and various kinds of supporting constructions.

■ Destroyed Forms

Destroyed forms are so named because they are destroyed in order to remove them from under the paper covering. The best-known example is a balloon used for the layering technique. A rubber ball is more suitable for making a round shape

from pulp because it is firmer. If more than half of the ball is covered, it will also have to be cut up.

■ Lost Forms

A lost form is not modelled but rather wrapped. Disposable objects made of thin, light material that will not disintegrate—for example, tin cans, cardboard cups, and plastic containers—are well suited to this method. The forms must usually be covered on both sides so that they are no longer visible.

To be excruciatingly precise, we cannot speak of pure paper mache when referring to this method, because other materials are also used.

■ Reusable Forms

Reusable forms need to be separated from the paper mache shell in one piece. In certain cases, the paper covering must be cut to achieve this.

Bowls, vases, pitchers, plates, cups, and bottles made of glass or porcelain are very suitable, as are enameled containers. They will not be damaged by cutting around them. Forms made of metal, wood, or plastic could be scratched.

Again, you must cover these forms with a lubricant to make it possible to separate them. Layered paper mache creates fewer problems when separating from a form because it is more flexible. Paper mache from pulp is advisable only for open forms such as bowls.

Forms II:
Homemade Forms and Supporting Structures

■ *Cardboard Constructions*

Cardboard constructions can be used for modelling or as lost forms. Use a reusable cardboard form for modelling a cone (page 62). In contrast, the cardboard frame of a teddy bear is a lost form; it is padded and remains inside the body (page 148). Many cardboard constructions, such as the picture frames on page 126 and the angular bowl on page 76, could be called cardboard craft. They too disappear inside the object.

Heavy pasteboard can be used for straight-edged cardboard frames. Corrugated cardboard is also appropriate, because it is light and stable at the same time. Corrugated cardboard should always be cut with a knife, because shears will crush the wavy parts. Forms with bent or folded sections can also be made from poster board and Bristol board.

Reusable cardboard constructions for modelling need to be covered with waterproof paper, because they are exposed to moisture for a long time. The most useful paper is book wrap—a clear, self-adhesive paper often used to wrap around books to protect them. Cardboard forms that will be covered with layers of paper and will disappear into the finished project can be protected with a coat of varnish.

You can model reusable cardboard frames with either pulp or layered paper. On the other hand, it is advisable to use

Forms III:
Plaster Forms

only the layering technique on lost cardboard forms, because covering them with pulp is problematic. Stresses and warping occur because the pulp shrinks too much.

Wire Constructions

You can cover wire constructions, whether hollow or not, entirely with a layer of paper; thus they are considered lost forms. You can work with structures made from simple wire that has been bent in a variety of ways.

A wire frame that is covered with a thin layer of paper has a light, linear character. You can make delicate stands to support all types of containers in this way. A stable construction made from 12 gauge (2 mm) zinc-coated steel wire serves as the core (see page 94 and following).

If the wire core is padded with a thick, crumpled layer of paper, the form takes on a massive appearance. This method was used for the Octopus Stands on page 98.

A wire frame can also determine the outline of a figure, an abstract object, or a container. In this case, it is covered tightly with paper. The paper layer can be so thin

that the wires stand out or are visible, as with the Dragon on page 152 and the Shield on page 172.

Constructions made of chicken wire are very good, especially for large figures or objects. The wire surfaces are cut and bent where needed. Individual pieces can be secured together with other pieces of wire. It is possible to push in or pull out the wire structure in order to compress or enlarge the form. For very large pieces, it may be necessary to build a wooden frame to support the chicken wire.

As a rule, chicken wire frames are enclosed by the object as lost forms. Only in a few cases, for example the Spirit Houses on page 170, is it possible to bend the wire structure and remove it from the paper covering. It is quite difficult to cover wire frames with pulp, as there are almost no surfaces for it to stick to. For this reason, pulp paper mache is not suitable for wire frames.

There is a trick to pasting paper on top of wire: whenever possible, paste the paper strips completely around once so that the end attaches to the beginning. Continue working by always attaching the edge of one paper strip to the next.

Another possibility is to paste paper simultaneously on both the inside and outside of the wire frame and in this way to fasten two layers of paper together.

Models of Clay or Plasticine

You can use your own imagination to create forms and then model them using the layering technique. Two-dimensional forms, masks, and medium-size free-standing forms are well suited. The clay form does not need to dry, but it must be covered with lubricant. Cover the clay form as before with strips of tissue paper; the more detailed the form, the smaller the scraps of paper. The clay form shrinks when it dries, which makes removing it easier. Reliefs can usually be separated in one piece from the paper shell, but three-dimensional forms must be cut off. The clay model is destroyed in the process. Bits of remaining clay can be scraped out of the paper covering. Dried clay can be kneaded and reused.

Plasticine is used exactly as described for clay. It is probably better suited for smaller objects. It does not shrink and dry out, so it is easier to re-use.

Three-dimensional details that are attached to the object and then covered with paper can also be made from clay or plasticine. In certain cases the modelling material gets stuck to the paper shell. It must either be removed carefully with a knife or the paper form cut off (page 50). Models of clay or plasticine are better for the layering technique than for pulp, because the details can be formed more distinctly.

The clay models that have just been described are positive forms, which are covered from the outside. Plaster casts made from positive forms such as these are negative forms. They are modelled from the inside. Plaster casts such as these can be used as often as you like.

There are few limits in shaping clay forms, because the paper covering is cut off and the clay model can be destroyed. But if a plaster cast is made from a clay model, there are more restrictions. The clay mold cannot remain inside the plaster cast. For that reason it cannot have any convex curves, where the clay would get stuck inside the plaster cast.

The clay model is placed on a work area, coated with vegetable oil, and then covered with plaster of Paris. When the plaster cast hardens, the clay form can be removed. What results is a hollow block of plaster.

The plaster cast must be sealed with varnish and carefully brushed with petroleum jelly or hand cream. Then you can cover it with pulp or paste on small pieces of paper. Pulp is better suited than the layering technique in this case. There is a detailed description of working with plaster molds, together with an example of a wall relief, on page 122.

Assembling Separate Pieces

Creating containers from paper mache is not limited to modelling balls, cones, and so on. It really begins to get interesting when something new is created by combining various elements from available forms.

There are several steps in putting individual pieces together.

■ Measuring and Marking

In order to join together two sections of a form—for example, a hemisphere and a cone—both parts must be measured and cut exactly to fit.

Use a compass to mark the edges of the sphere and cone shapes. The compass can be used on a spherical shape from either the inside or the outside. While the middle point of a cone is obvious, it has to be determined on a hemisphere (half a sphere). Using a measuring tape, measure across the hemisphere twice to find the mid-point (see illustration). Measure and mark straight parts with a ruler as usual.

■ Cutting

Cutting a paper shell can be done accurately with a sharp craft knife. The cutting line is first drawn in pencil, then traced with the knife and cut lightly. Pierce the paper shell with the knife point, then draw the blade along the line.

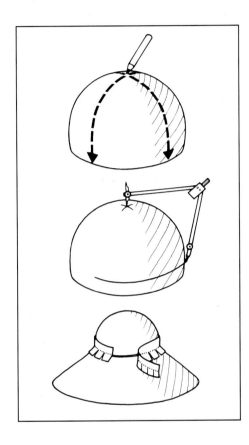

A shell of pulp cannot be separated with one cut. You must move the knife along the cutting line often enough to cut through. You can also use a small saw with a fine blade used for metal to make straight cuts.

■ Gluing

Join the two pieces by applying wood glue along the cut edges and joining the pieces so they fit exactly. Secure the pieces with tape until they dry. Paste strips of pa-per onto the underside of the seam. Later, remove the tape and then paste paper strips onto the front side as well.

You can strengthen a seam by pasting a strip of cloth saturated with wood glue onto the underside of it. When gluing a rounded surface, cut the cloth strips at right angles to the edge (see illustration). Later, cover the cloth strips with paper.

To reassemble paper shells that have been cut apart in order to remove the form after modelling, glue the two cut edges together. Secure the parts in the correct positions until they are dry with rubber bands or tape.

When the object is assembled and the glue is dry, use sandpaper or a file to smooth out the rough edges. Uneven places or places where parts are joined can be evened out with a little putty (page 22). Cover these areas with a layer of paper.

Thick-walled pieces made from pulp are easy to glue together. Cover the broad, cut surfaces with glue on both sides and join them together. Wipe away any glue that oozes out. If you cover the seam with a little bit of pulp, the object will look as though it is all one piece.

2

Bowls From Balloons

The next three chapters are about containers made of paper mache, beginning with bowls of layered paper modelled on balloons. This simplest of all paper mache techniques, which many of us learned in kindergarten, is the point of departure for lovely, varied designs.

- *Simple Spherical Bowls*

- *Bowls With Segmented Rims*

- *Bowls With Rims and Bases*

- *A Double-Walled Bowl*

- *Two Lens-Shaped Bowls*

- *Small, Oval Bowls*

- *Irregular Vessel*

Simple Spherical Bowls

Spherical bowls are an ideal introduction to the world of paper mache, because you can learn the basic technique quickly and easily as you make them. Also, the sphere is one of the most beautiful and balanced basic forms. You can choose a hemisphere (half a sphere) or a larger or smaller portion of the sphere.

Like almost every object made of paper mache, these bowls require a master form on which to work. Balloons and balls will serve admirably.

Working with balloons is especially easy. After finishing your project, you can simply pierce the balloon, and it almost automatically separates from the paper shell. (For complete instructions for layering on a balloon, see Chapter 1, page 14.)

Although balloons tend to be oval, they are suitable forms for hemispheres. For an exactly round form, you should use a ball. Of course, if you cover more than half the ball, then you must destroy it in order to remove it.

If you want to make a spherical bowl from paper mache, you should almost certainly use a ball. A balloon would yield to pressure too readily.

I made the bowls shown in the photo in order to learn about the properties of various types of paper. The types used here are good to work with to greater or lesser degrees.

I like to work with strong tissue paper best, using white tissue for the first three layers and for the last three. The white outer layers cover up any printing that might be on the inner layers.

The character of the paper shows up most beautifully if you use a glaze paint on it. The reddish pink bowl has been rubbed with a thin coat of oil paint.

The turquoise blue bowl is made of Ingres paper. It demonstrates clearly that this high-quality paper, available in many beautiful colors, is unfortunately very hard to work with because it is relatively heavy and, for that reason, inflexible. You must tear it into very small pieces to avoid creases.

The thin white bowl is made of a few layers of kite paper and is slightly opaque. Even a few layers result in a very firm, parchment-like consistency, which nevertheless becomes a bit creased when dry. It also tends to warp.

The thick-walled white bowl is made from pulp. The basic material is facial tissue, and the form is a ball, which was half-covered with layers of paper. You can orient yourself easily by the distinct seam of the ball. If you cover only half the ball, you can remove it easily because you can squeeze it together. (You will find further instructions for making and working with pulp in Chapter 1, pages 16-22.)

Bowls With Segmented Rims

Like all the projects in this chapter, these two bowls are made from balloons, using the layering technique. They are among my favorite things, largely because they are created so simply yet effectively from a simple spherical shape.

For the blue bowl, layer your paper over a portion of the balloon. When the paper shell is finished, mark the rim with a compass and then cut if off cleanly.

Paint the bowl before continuing to work on it. Apply a thin coat of Prussian blue artist's oil paint to a cloth and rub it onto the outside of the bowl. For the inside, apply a primer of pink acrylic paint. Then rub on a coat of carmine red oil paint. The primer causes the red to develop a greater luminosity. The oil paint is easier to work with if you add a drop of turpentine substitute.

To create the segmented rim, draw a line on the inside of the bowl 1½ inches (4 cm) from the edge. Using a craft knife, press gently along the line on the inside to make a groove. Cut vertically into the strip of edging approximately every ¾ inch (2 cm) (see illustration). Then carefully bend the individual segments inward.

If you like, you can embellish the segmented rim. Every segment of the blue bowl has a piece of yellow kite paper pasted around it so that it juts out to the left a

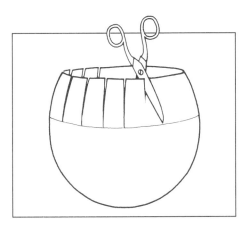
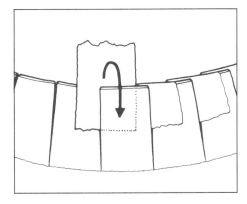
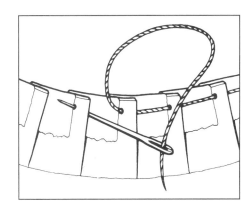

bit (see illustration). Push each yellow end inward (so that it is behind the segment to its left) and sew the individual segments together with yarn (see illustration).

The brown bowl was created in the same way, except the segmented rim is much wider. The lower part approximates a hemisphere; figure about 4 inches (10 cm) for the rim. Do not cut the edge, but rather tear it in a slightly jagged line while it is still moist.

Stain the outside of the bowl with brown wood stain; paint the inside carmine red, as described above. Cut the broad rim of the brown bowl in segments about 2 inches (5 cm) wide.

The decoration on this bowl consists of simple indigo-colored triangles, which divide the segments diagonally. The colorfulness and simple geometric flatness are reminiscent of Indian terra cotta.

Bowls With Rims and Bases

Round bowls can be enhanced with various details. The bowls shown here were placed on bases and given flat rims. The rim makes the bowl stronger and allows for good stability.

Putting together separate patterns for sphere, rim, and base allows you to play with the proportions. You can choose various spherical forms. The curve of the bowl can be flat or deep. The width of the rim can vary, and the base can be straight or cone-shaped. The sketches at right show how containers with completely different characteristics can result from the same basic elements.

Creating these two bowls is very simple. For both of them you use a balloon for the round form. Draw the upper edge of the layered paper bowl with a compass at the desired height, but do not cut it yet.

Using the compass again, draw the rim on heavy pasteboard. The inner diameter of the rim is the circumference of the bowl divided by 3.14. Cut the rim using a craft knife and place it onto the round form until it sits firmly.

Attach the rim of the orange-green bowl on the underside with a strip of cloth saturated with wood glue. After it is dry, cut the top of the bowl so that it is flush with the flat rim. Finally, paste paper strips onto both sides of the rim to cover up the seam. The rim of the golden bowl was not pasted to the bowl but rather stitched on with brass wire. The bowl was cut off 3/8 inch (1 cm) above the rim.

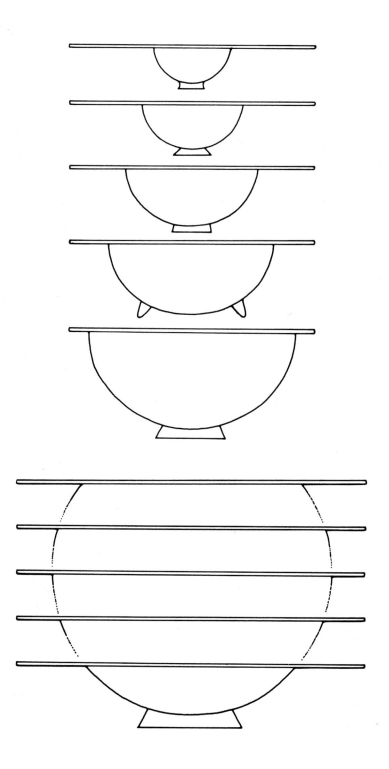

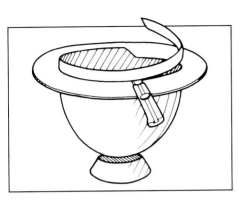

Both bowls have a cone-shaped base, which consists of a small cone that has been cut down. (For instructions on making a cone, see page 62.) An alternative would be a straight base from a piece of a cardboard tube. Glue the base on from the inside.

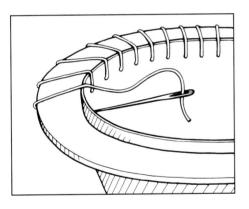

To create the orange-green serrated pattern, coat the piece with acrylic paint in orange and turquoise. Blend the colors by rubbing on a very thin coat of azure in umber. Add a speckled effect by dipping a toothbrush in the paint, then flicking it on the bowl.

Apply a primer coat of dark blue on the golden bowl and then gild it. (For gilding instructions, see page 196.) Keep the rim blue and apply clear varnish; this is under the gold. Finally, sew the rim together with thin brass wire (see illustration).

A Double-Walled Bowl

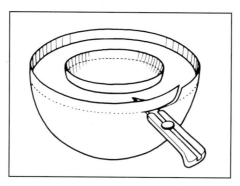

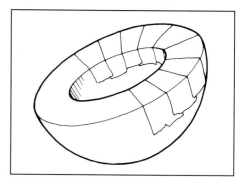

This double-walled bowl is a sphere-sphere combination. A small sphere floats in a larger one; they are held together by a common rim.

There are many possibilities for playing with the relative size of the two spheres, making the hollow space broader or narrower as a result. (See the illustrations below.) Both spheres may have a common middle point but do not need to.

Depending on whether you cut the sphere lower or higher, the resulting bowls can be open and flat, or higher and more rounded. The rim joining them can be flat, conical, or more vertical.

The model shown here consists of two large hemispheres that have a common middle point and that are joined together with a flat rim. The hemispheres were modeled on balloons. The crushed texture of the outer bowl came about because the balloon shrank while the paper covering was still moist, resulting in creases.

Mark the upper edge of each bowl but do not cut them off yet. First make the rim of heavy cardboard. Measure the circumference of the larger bowl, divide it by 3.14, and draw a circle of that diameter on the cardboard, using a compass. Repeat with the smaller bowl, drawing that circle inside

the first. Now cut out the cardboard rim.

Paste a narrow strip of corrugated cardboard inside the large bowl exactly underneath the desired level of the rim. Cover the upper edge of the corrugated cardboard with a thick layer of glue.

Push the smaller bowl into the opening of the rim so that it sits firmly and glue it securely from the inside. Then push the rim inside the outer bowl until it sits on the strip of corrugated cardboard. You may cut away the parts of both bowls that extend above the rim after they are dry. As a final step, glue paper strips over the rim so that the seams are covered.

Gild the outside of the bowl on top of the green background and then polish it a bit. (For details about gilding, see page 196.) Rub the rim and the inside with reddish-grey oil paint.

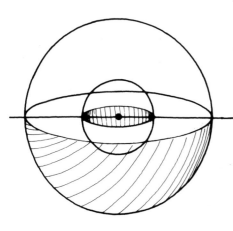

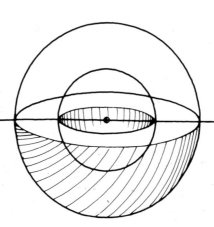

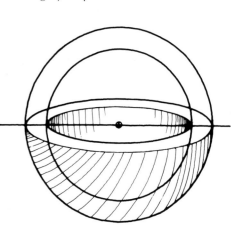

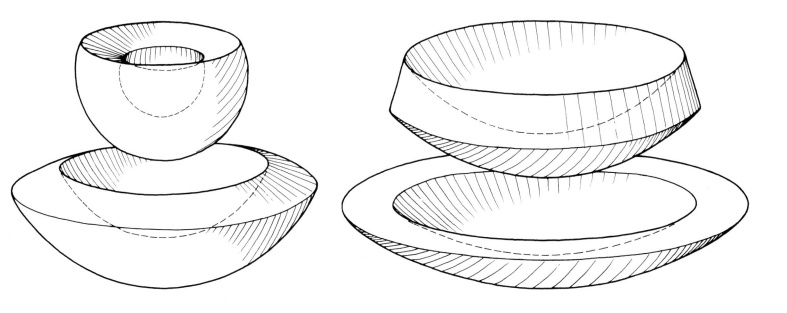

Two Lens-Shaped Bowls

As their name implies, these two bowls are created from lens-shaped hollow bodies into which openings are cut in various ways. This is another possibility for combining round forms with one another.

The lens form consists of two equal round sections placed together. The flatter you cut the spheres, the flatter the lens will be.

For the green bowl, blow up two balloons to equal size and paste paper strips on them, using the layering technique. It is sufficient to cover the upper third of each balloon. Mark both halves equally, using a compass, and then cut them. Mark the bowl's opening also and cut it out with a scalpel or a very sharp knife. This is easier to manage if done before assembling the parts.

Then join the two halves together with tape at several places so that they fit together exactly. Spread wood glue in the area between the cut edges, then cover the seam with narrow paper strips.

Glue a string along the seam in order to highlight the lens shape, then cover this seam with two additional layers of paper. It is advisable to spread a little glue along the edges where the opening was cut in order to protect it.

Cover the entire upper surface uniformly with one type of white paper. Then rub in a very thin mixture of floor wax and oil paint in emerald green. Different types of paper can take on different shades of the color. The green color mainly sticks to the torn edges of the paper and results in a delicate random pattern. In addition, you

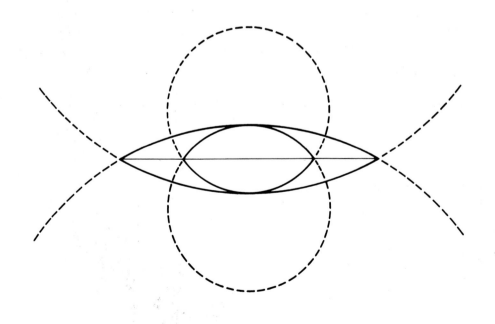

can decorate the upper side of the bowl with a thick, white cord sewn on with green embroidery floss.

The patterned, lens-shaped bowl is a lens form cut in half and stood vertically on end. You will need to cover only a third of the balloon with paper layers. Draw a flat bowl form with a compass and divide it into two equal halves. Then attach both parts to their former outer rims (see the illustration). This process has been described earlier.

As you can see in the photo, the rims curve a little inward, because of the surface tensions that can result when a round body is cut.

The decoration on the two lens-shaped bowls results from the application of various colors, which are then partially rubbed off. This technique allows irregular patterns to emerge on the uneven background. (For more information on this technique, see page 188.)

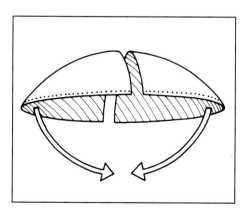

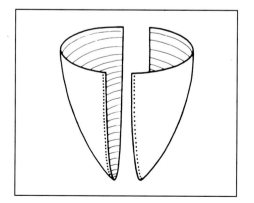

Small Oval Bowl and Irregular Bowl

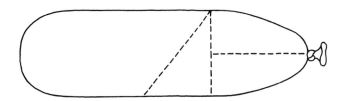

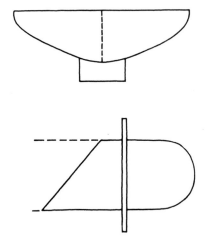

These very different objects have in common the fact that they are both created out of portions of a long balloon. One modelling is sufficient to make both bowls.

For the small oval bowl, use the narrow, tapering end of the paper shell formed down by the balloon's knot. Cut that piece straight across, then again down the middle axis. Glue the two halves together at the round cut surfaces. Set the bowl on a small cylindrical base that fits exactly to the shape of the bowl (a ring cut from a cardboard tube will do) and attach the base with wood glue. To finish, paste tissue paper over all seams.

Coat the upper surface of the small bowl with a mixture of grainy putty, glue, and white paint, and add a touch of color with red clay. (For details about decorating techniques using clay, see page 190.)

The irregularly shaped container for writing utensils is made from the round end of the balloon and a cardboard ring. The angle creates a center of gravity for it, so the container balances on its ring whether or not it is full.

Begin with the cardboard ring. Measure the circumference of the balloon, divide it by 3.14, and draw a circle that diameter on the cardboard, using a compass. Decide how wide you want the rim to be, then draw a circle outside the first one, placing the point of the compass exactly in the center of the first circle. Cut out the ring, cutting the inside opening a bit too narrow at first; correct this later, after you have positioned the ring so that it is firmly seated.

Now cut the balloon on the diagonal. The diagonal angle is even if it touches a flat surface everywhere. Mark the position of the ring on the balloon and cover it with glue. Then press the ring into place. Cover the seam and outer surface of the cardboard ring with several layers of paper.

The decoration of the irregularly shaped container is enlivened by the contrast of rough and shiny surfaces. Coat the outside with rough putty and the surfaces that will be handled with white primer; then polish and cover with shellac.

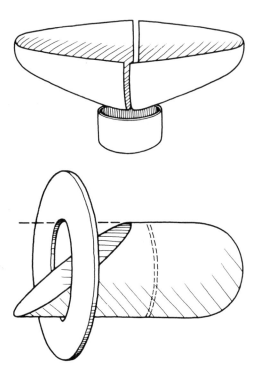

3

Modelling on Everyday Objects

This chapter deals with modelling on common solid objects—for example, bowls, bottles, and cans. They serve as basic forms for your own designs. An object can be transformed by interesting decoration alone, or it can take on a new, distinct appearance by adding details.

- *Orange Paper Mache Bowl*

- *Two-Toned Paper Mache Bowl*

- *Animals and Dots on Layered Bowls*

- *Making Feet for a Bowl*

- *Vases and Amphora*

- *Two Goblets*

- *Transforming a Soup Can*

- *A Four-Footed Can*

Orange Paper Mache Bowl, or a Butterfly Dances in the Rain

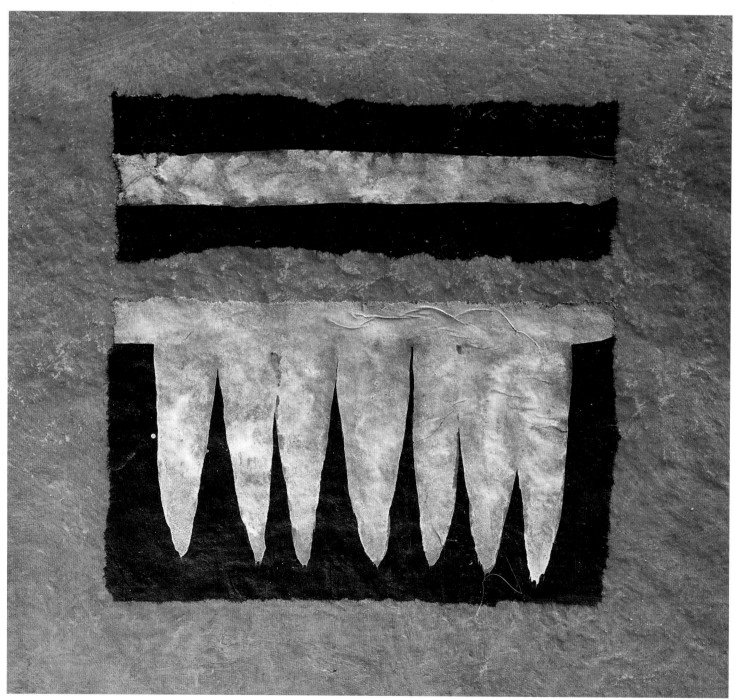

The many-faceted attraction of modelling on everyday containers lies first of all in the area of decoration. An entire palette of techniques is available, allowing you to make use of every imaginable type of design: figures, ornamental and abstract motifs, and geometric shapes. Motifs can be used singly or repeatedly; they can form rows of patterns or be scattered about.

The bowl shown is made of pulp modelled on the inside of a large glass bowl. The pulp would have fit too tightly if done around the outside of the bowl; separating the pulp would have been too difficult because of its rigidity.

First apply lubricant to the inside of the glass bowl. Then spread the pulp evenly on the surface. Press the mass down carefully and firmly, and work with it so that you get a homogeneous layer; otherwise, tears or air pockets could result underneath the paper mache. Finally, smooth out the entire surface with a spoon, which is better suited than a knife for a concave surface. For this bowl I used pulp with added flour; the recipe is on page 21.

It may take a week for the bowl to dry. When it does, it will be easy to release, since it will shrink.

Round off the rim of the bowl a little with a rasp (a flat wood file) and smooth out the entire surface with emery paper.

Pulp with added flour becomes very hard and is easy to work with.

The decoration on the bowl is an orange-colored acrylic glaze onto which the individual motifs are pasted. The motifs are painted on tissue paper primed in black and then torn out. I did not use black tissue paper, because it fades. The outer motifs symbolize clouds from which rain is falling; there is a butterfly in the middle. As a final step, coat the bowl with a clear matte varnish to protect it.

Two-Toned Paper Mache Bowl

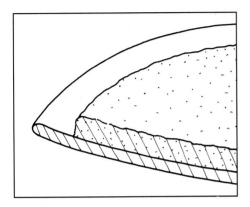 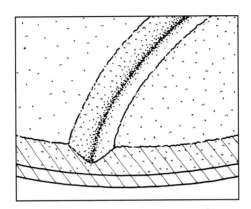 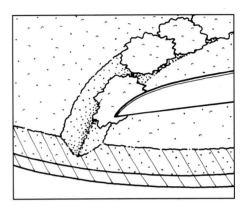

The bowl shown here is made of pulp modeled on a large, very flat glass bowl. The unusual thing about it is the working of the paper mache in two tones. The pulp is a mixture of violet paper napkins and white typing paper.

Coat the inside of the glass bowl with a lubricant, then cover it entirely with pulp. Work the pulp into an even layer and smooth it out with a spoon or a similar implement. Form the rim so that the paper mache only comes to within about ¹/₂ inch (1 cm) of the rim of the glass bowl all the way around.

The second step is to work the white pattern into the violet surface. First draw pattern lines by making a furrow in the surface with your finger. Do not break through the layer of paper mache when doing this; just push down gently. Fill this furrow with small lumps of white pulp a little at a time. Straighten out the little lumps with a knife and distribute them evenly (see illustration).

Carefully flatten the patterned surface and then smooth it out with a knife. Finally, fill in the area not covered around the rim of the glass bowl with white pulp.

It takes a while for the paper mache to dry out. The flatter the bowl, the greater the danger that the paper mache will become warped while drying. Thus, it is wise to keep an eye on the drying process and, in case parts begin to bulge, weight them down. If necessary, you can moisten the paper mache and place it in the bowl form again.

When working with paper mache of different colors, you will naturally think of placing various types of pulp next to each other. Unfortunately, my experience has been that the pulp does not stick together well enough, and gaps develop between the different colors when it dries. Thus I consider it is wise to apply different types of pulp onto one basic foundation used to hold everything together. This base can be made of pulp, as described above, or from a strong layer of pasted strips of paper.

47

Animals and Dots on Layered Bowls

Using layered paper mache for bowls opens up the possibility of applying the strips on the inside or the outside. Each side has advantages and disadvantages.

Use the layering technique on the outside of bowls with awkward bases or uneven exterior surfaces. In unfortunate cases, the paper layers come apart when drying and leave gaps. To avoid this, carefully press out all possible air bubbles and improve the adhesive quality of the paste with wood glue. Shrinkage while drying does have the positive effect of making it easier to release the form.

Both of these projects were done by layering on large, flat bowls. Don't forget to coat the bowl with a lubricant or to moisten the first two layers with water only.

The blue bowl has a narrow rim bent outward, which gives it its perfect shape, as well as greater stability. Therefore it must have the paper layers applied on the inside. Press downward repeatedly on the paper strips that extend out beyond the rim so that they end up pointing outward from the rim.

After the paper bowl is dry, cut the material that overlaps the rim so that about $\frac{1}{2}$ inch (1 cm) remains. When releasing the bowl from the form, you must temporarily bend it upward somewhat to be able to grasp it underneath. Paste either some string or, even better, a thick wire onto the fold in order to strengthen the rim. Then paste narrow paper strips over the rim.

This bowl is decorated with a random pattern of animal figures. It is made of paper layers worked in a sandwich fashion. In that way the motifs are enclosed between the background and the final layer of paper (see also page 193).

It does not matter whether the dotted bowl is modeled on the inside or the outside of the form. Trim the edge straight and add a flat rim of cardboard. Trim it on the inside so that the rim and the bowl fit together exactly. Finally, cover the pasted seam with several layers of paper.

The decoration defines the surface of the bowl in two areas and highlights its rim. The pattern is applied with hot wax

or latex onto the white paper background and then covered with colored wood stain or liquid acrylic paint. The wax-covered parts do not take on the paint. You will find more about the resist method on page 187.

Making Feet for a Bowl

These two projects are also formed from everyday objects. Because they have additional details and are double-walled, they give the appearance of being massive. Both containers were made in the same way, so it will suffice to describe the light blue one.

The bowls were made using a technique in which the feet and handles were integrated into the form, rather than added on later. They were made from plasticine and attached to the bowl. In order for the feet to turn out equal in size, divide the plasticine into seven equal portions, form the feet from these portions, and then set them onto the base of the bowl equidistant apart. Their conical shape makes the removal of the plasticine easier later. Place the bowl carefully on its feet and check whether it is level. Model the handles from plasticine as well, and position them on so that they fit the shape of rim.

Paste paper strips on both the inside and outside of the bowl. To do that, first place the bowl on a suitable base that will allow you to rotate it easily. Then coat the outside with lubricant and apply three layers of paper onto the outside. Turn the

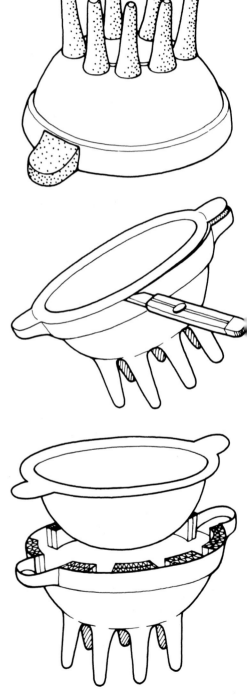

bowl over, coat the inside with lubricant, and paste layers of paper on the inside. Continue to apply paper, alternating inside and out, until there are 10 layers.

Cut the paper shell off after it is dry. The cutting line must run along the outer edge of the rim and the handles (see illustration). Run a knife under the upper half of the handle and lift the inner shell up. It will be easy to release.

Before releasing the outer shell, remove the plasticine from the handles. Loosen the paper shell with a knife. Now take firm hold of the bowl in the area where the handle is joined, and at the

same time pull and gently move the legs back and forth to loosen the plasticine from the bottom of the bowl. Repeat this on both sides until the sections come apart. It is helpful to cut a small hole in the bottom of the bowl to prevent a vacuum. Finally, you must separate the plasticine from the feet. Try using a corkscrew!

Before assembling the paper sections, prepare padding from several layers of corrugated cardboard. Attach the padding firmly onto the base and along the sides of the outer shell to create some space between the inner and outer shells (see illustration). Apply glue to the inner shell when

it is positioned properly, then glue it into place.

The light blue bowl has a brown pattern painted on it. Inspired by American Indian motifs, it shows a cat pursuing a bird, and stylized butterflies. A procedure described on page 198 can lend the bowl a worn look.

To finish the three-footed bowl, apply black acrylic paint over the entire surface. Apply shellac on the outside and rub orange-red powdered clay to the inside (careful, it stains!).

Vase and Amphora

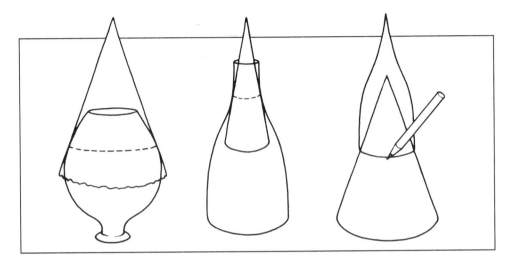

■ *Modelling Bottles*

First cover the bottle with a lubricant to keep the paper from sticking, or form the first two layers with paper that has been dipped in water. Then continue covering the bottle with about 15 layers of tissue paper. After the paper shell has dried, it will fit so tightly around the bottle that you will have to cut it along one side to release it.

Spread wood glue on the cut edges and join them together again. In addition, glue narrow paper strips to the inner and outer sides of the seam. Place the shell loosely over the bottle again while it is drying so that it does not get misshapen from moisture at any one spot.

The vase and the amphora are reminiscent of ancient containers and require stands to hold them. These are created from molds of bottles combined with

cones. These two projects, as well as the goblets, should actually be included in the next chapter because of the cones, but I find that they fit better here because their interesting shapes are mainly the result of the bottle form.

Use a narrow wine bottle for the vase. In addition, a larger and a small, narrow cone are needed. The cone is made with the help of a cardboard form. Exact instructions are found on page 60. The bottle shape is somewhat shortened at the bottom.

Place the small cone inside the bottle-shaped shell so that it sticks out of the neck opening. Cut the opening back far enough to create a transition from one piece to the other that is not too obvious. Then attach the cone to the inside with wood glue. Put the resulting piece onto the larger cone and cut the cone to fit. Spread wood glue on the cut edges and glue them together; cover the seams with paper strips.

A bottle is also used for the amphora— in this case, a rounded wine bottle. A similarly shaped vase could be used as a substitute. Only one cone is needed for the amphora.

Place the cone over the upended bottle shell and cut it down so that none of the cone still sticks out over the edge of the bottle. When it sits well, cover the inside with wood glue and glue it on. After the glue is well hardened, use a file to smooth the point where the two shapes are joined and cover it with paper.

The upper surface of both projects is made of very thin, transparent, yellow kite paper, and has carmine red oil paint rubbed onto the surface. A subtle but strong orange tone results. The torn edges of the paper strips also stand out, forming an interesting texture, because they absorb more paint.

Both stands are made of wire covered with paper. The process of making the wire stand is described on page 94.

Two Goblets

These goblets are combinations of bottles and cones. The shape of the goblet is determined primarily by the shape of the bottle used. Use a Bordeaux wine bottle with the very narrow curve in its neck for the green goblet and a mineral water bottle with a conical neck for the red-blue goblet.

In addition to the bottles, you will need a large and a small cone. Place the three parts loosely on top of one another to determine how best to cut the bottle section and how large the cones should be.

If the proportions are correct, assemble the individual parts. I allowed the base

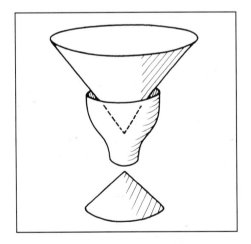

cone to extend into the bottle section. This style can be seen in old blown glass, and it looks very nice if you can see into the goblet. Cover the lower rim of the bottle section with glue and set the cone on it. Cut an opening in the upper cone that is just a bit too narrow and then glue the cone into the bottle section (see illustration). After it is dry, trim the excess. Cover all seams with paper.

Pieces of string and miniature cones decorate the outside of the goblets. Paste narrow strips of paper over the decorations, to give the surface a unified character.

Prime both goblets with acrylic paint and then cover them with an oil glaze. Mix the acrylic color so that it is several shades lighter than the color of the next layer of glaze.

You may gild the object only after the oil varnish is thoroughly dry; otherwise, the gold will stick to parts where you do not want it to. Brush size on all parts that are to be gilded or covered with silver leaf: the inside of the green goblet, the small decorative cones, and the string on the red and blue goblet. The small gold leaves will stick to the size later when it is almost dry. You can wipe it off the other parts later. See page 196 for complete gilding instructions.

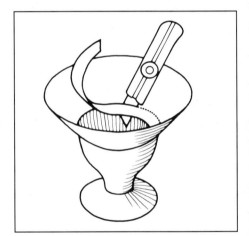

Transformation of a Soup Can

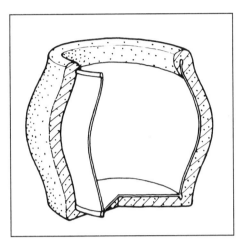
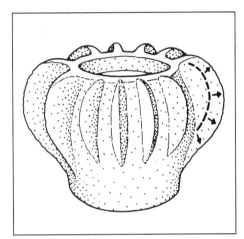

The attraction of using everyday objects is that you can reproduce just about any available object in paper mache. Moreover, these everyday objects can be inspiration for your own designs. You can enhance, alter, or decorate the form of the object in a variety of ways.

The simplest way of working with everyday objects is to treat them as lost forms so that you do not have the problem of removing them. For the most part, only light containers with thin walls are suitable for this. Plastic containers of all types, from the margarine container to the shampoo bottle, and tin cans of the most diverse shapes, from the small savings box to the tuna can, are ideal. Containers of glass, ceramic, or porcelain are too thick and heavy; they don't capture the character of the paper mache well at all.

Hidden inside the segmented container shown here is a large, rounded soup can imported from Europe. It was covered with paper mache and then enhanced with decorative elements also of paper mache.

The transformation of the soup can takes place in two steps. You need just barely half of the entire amount of pulp for the first step. Cover the outside and bottom of the can with it. Spread it evenly on the surface and press it flat. Add a little more above the upper rim toward the inside, so that the rim is covered.

For the next step, divide the rest of the pulp into 11 equal portions. You will form small, semicircular arches with these, placing the 11 portions equidistant from one another. Coat the surface where you will attach them with glue so they will stick bet-

ter. Press them on firmly and smooth down firmly the places where they join the can. Then carefully press each individual arch flat, using your fingers; this makes the thin segments larger. Finally, cover the segments with a thin coat of paste so that you can create a smooth surface on the paper mache. It makes your work easier if you place the can upside down on top of another container or base to support it, so you can rotate it more easily.

Either paste paper on the inside of the can or coat it with a mixture of pulp, wood glue, and a little water. After it is dry, color the segmented can entirely with an acrylic glaze in a dull blue-green. In this way the rough texture of the paper mache is preserved.

Four-Footed Can

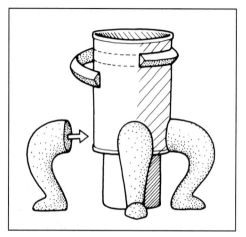
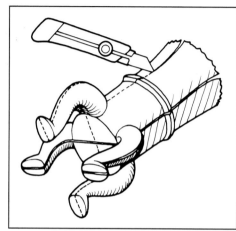
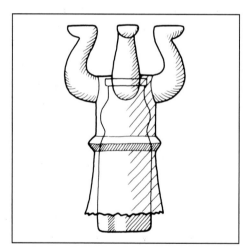
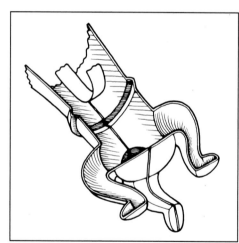

This container is molded on a tin can, with the details done in plasticine. Thus the feet were not added on later but were covered with layers of paper together with the can, as part of the same process. For that reason they are hollow and seem to be outgrowths of the entire form.

The first step is to attach the feet to the can. Divide the plasticine into five equal portions, reserving the fifth portion for later.

Model the feet from the four portions and press them onto the can. Use an object of the same height as a support for the can so that the feet do not bend (see illustration). Now check whether the feet are attached symmetrically and are uniform in shape.

The rest of the plasticine is for two purposes. First, add a decorative strip in relief to the upper area of the can (see illustration). Secondly, even out the seam between the bottom of the can and the bottom itself so that the paper shell does not get stuck on it later.

Cover the entire form with lubricant before covering it with paper. The first layer of paper on the inside will be visible later; on this project, I used thin packing paper. Allow the paper strips to extend out

over the edge of the can. Extend the rim further and further out, layer by layer.

For covering the legs and feet, turn the piece upside down onto a juice bottle so that the delicate rim is not harmed. The paper has to be torn into very small pieces for the curved parts on the legs and feet. After the first layer, continue with 12 additional layers. The last layer is packing paper again. The rim should have grown about 4 inches (10 cm) out beyond the upper edge of the can; it bends slightly outward and is very thin at the ends.

After it is dry, you must cut the paper shell to release it. Divide the container into two symmetrical axes, each of which runs through the middle of the feet in four equal parts (see illustration). Cut the legs diagonally through the plasticine so that you can use a knife blade along the gap and lift the parts out. The segments will now come out.

To join together all the parts of the shell again, first join the quarters into halves and then these into the whole (see illustration). Coat the cut edges with wood glue and join the edges together. Use tape to hold the parts together until they dry. Finally, cover as many seams as you can reach with paper on both sides.

4

Containers From Homemade Structures

Simple frameworks made of cardboard make it possible for you to choose the shape you want the container to take. In this chapter I will introduce simple supporting constructions that are geometrical or free-form. Many cardboard forms can be used over and over again; others disappear inside the container.

- *Making Cones*

- *Groups of Cones*

- *Sphere-Cone Combinations*

- *Bowls From Half Cones*

- *A Double-Cone Bowl*

- *Bowls From Pyramids*

- *A Pyramid on Legs*

- *Two Rectangular Baskets*

- *A Diagonal Tray on Two Feet*

- *Bear Bowl*

Making Cones

Since there are no ready-made forms on which to model paper mache cones, you must make the form yourself. In the following section, I will call a supporting structure such as this a "working cone."

Draw a circle on a large sheet of flexible cardboard with a radius somewhat larger than the planned cone. Cut it out and then cut into the circle up to the middle. Carefully slice off one layer of the cardboard along the cut edge so that it will not be too thick at the seam later. Form the circle into a cone with the desired size opening and secure it with paper clips. Secure the seam with a broad strip of tape. Cover this working cone with waterproof book paper to keep it from getting wet.

You can also make a variable working cone. The cardboard disc should have a radius of about 14 inches (35 cm). You can draw concentric circles on the disc as measuring points for cones of various sizes. In addition, mark several different angles, so that you can re-create a given angle of an opening later. The entire cardboard disc must be covered with waterproof paper. This working cone is now ready for use as needed in various situations; after you remove the adhesive tape and paper clips, you can store it flat.

Since the working cone is flexible and covered with waterproof paper, you will not need to apply lubricant. It is practical to set the cone onto a pot or bottle, de-

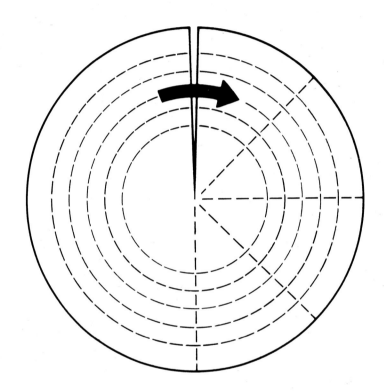

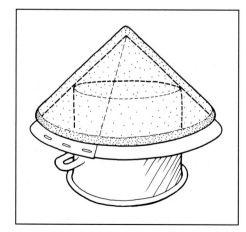

pending on whether it is shallow or narrow, in order to be able to rotate it while working on it.

Pasting on layers of paper is done as usual. The paper strips can be quite big, because the cone has no convex surfaces that might cause creases. If you tear the paper into cone-shaped pieces, they will fit nicely onto the cone form, and the work can progress quickly. After it dries, draw along the outer edge with a compass and trim the edge.

You can easily make cone forms of pulp as well. Working with pulp exerts a considerable amount of pressure on the supporting form. Resting the object on a pot helps prevent the working cone from bending. Do not trim the edges of objects made of pulp afterwards, but model them as in their finished state.

The bowl shown has a diameter of almost 20 inches (50 centimeters) and is made of white paper mache pulp.

Basically, cones need stands, whether pedestals or frames made of cardboard or wire. You will find ideas and instructions for these in the chapter on feet.

63

A Grouping of Cones

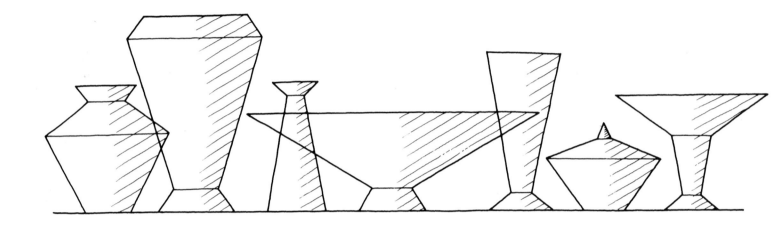

Besides spheres, cones have the most interesting possibilities for making containers in geometric shapes. Cone-cone combinations can be flat and open, high and narrow, or fat and rounded. Another possibility is to stack a large number of cones to form a column, which looks like lathe work. As with spheres, cones can be put together to form lovely containers.

The bowls shown here are very easy to make: cone-shaped bases support cone-shaped bowls. The cones are made of pulp, as described on the last page. The angle of the cone determines the proportions.

Cut off the tip of the base cone. In contrast, the larger bowl cone is not cut down and juts into the base. (The opposite would also be possible; then the tip of the base would jut into the bowl.) Glue the base onto the bowl with wood glue.

The slender, light blue vase is constructed from a tall, narrow cone and a smaller, broad cone. Both cones are covered using the layering technique.

Put the tall cone on top of the smaller one, going over the perimeter and cutting the tip to fit. Glue the two parts together

with wood glue. Glue a string to the outside of the rim as decoration. Paste paper strips over the seam and the string.

Paste white tissue paper over the surface for decoration. Apply the pattern onto the paper with wax and paint over it with light blue paint. More about the resist technique is found on page 187.

A wire stand must support this cone vase. Instructions for it are on page 95.

The Sphere-Cone Combination

Joining a cone and sphere is a natural because both forms are round. In addition to the two examples shown, there are other possible combinations that can be narrow or open at the top, such as rounded vases with conical necks.

The bowl without a rim is put together from two parts: a cone and a hemisphere. First determine the size of the sphere so that it fits onto the cone while leaving an unobtrusive area where the two are joined. Flatten out the rim of the cone from the inside, coat it with wood glue, and set it on the hemisphere. After the glue is dry, cut the opening into the cone form, first somewhat too small, then cut off the remainder to fit exactly. Now paste paper strips on both sides of the seam.

This bowl is covered on the outside with transparent yellow kite paper. The tip of the cone is emphasized by pasting layers of colored kite paper onto it. Decorate the rim on the inside and outside with a narrow black line.

The second bowl consists of a large and a small cone and a smaller hemisphere. Begin joining the hemisphere and the little cone as described above. The small cone disappears into the inside of the bowl and is given a broad rim.

For the rim of the container, make a very flat cone. Place the finished hemisphere-cone onto the flat cone and glue them together. Paste over the seam with strips of material soaked in glue, so that the parts stick together better (see illustration). After the glue hardens, sand the uneven spots until they are smooth. Then cut the opening in the cone and trim off the excess paper cleanly. Finally, paste over all seams on both sides.

This bowl is covered in a yellow and ocher-colored acrylic glaze; the inside is colored with an eggplant shade of oil paint. Apply a black-white decorative strip at an equal height all around the hemisphere.

Both bowls are supported by wire frames. Instructions for making such frames are found on page 94. The shapes of the components are shown in the drawings.

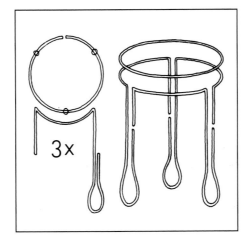

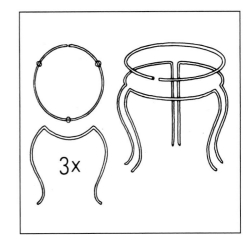

Bowls From Half Cones

If you cut a cone in half vertically and join the rounded sides together again, you get a rhomboid. You can vary the proportions of this container by changing the angle of the opening of the cone: long and narrow, or short and broad.

The narrow black bowl is made from a very narrow cone covered with paper layers. Place a mark on the rim of the cone, measure halfway around the circumference, and mark again. Draw a line from each mark to the tip of the cone, then cut the cone along these lines.

Place the cone on its cut edges and join together the two halves of the cone at the round edges. Assemble the parts in this position. Coat the edges with a little wood glue and cover the seam on the outside with a narrow strip of paper. After the seam is dry, smooth out the uneven areas. Cover the seam again with narrow strips of paper on the inside and outside.

The outside of this bowl is covered with black tissue paper. Since this fades after some time, I rubbed the surface with a mixture of black and ruby red oil paint. That gave the black a lovely eggplant-colored shimmer. The inside is pale blue with sprinkles of white. Along the inner seam is a black band with silver stripes. The rim is covered with silver as well.

The red and blue bowl is made of pulp. While making a paper mache cone, I was considering a simple conical bowl with a narrow rim. Later I decided to cut it up, and that resulted in the unusual double rim on the half-cone bowl. To join the halves, you need only to coat the edges with wood glue.

The outside of the bowl is a glaze of many layers of carmine red acrylic paint and shellac. Several coats of gesso were applied to the inside and sanded repeatedly until the surface was very smooth. Then a coat of indigo was applied and the surface polished. The rim, like that of the narrow bowl, is covered with silver. Further information about applying silver is found on page 196.

Both semi-conical bowls are supported by decorative wire stands. Instructions for making these stands are found on page 96.

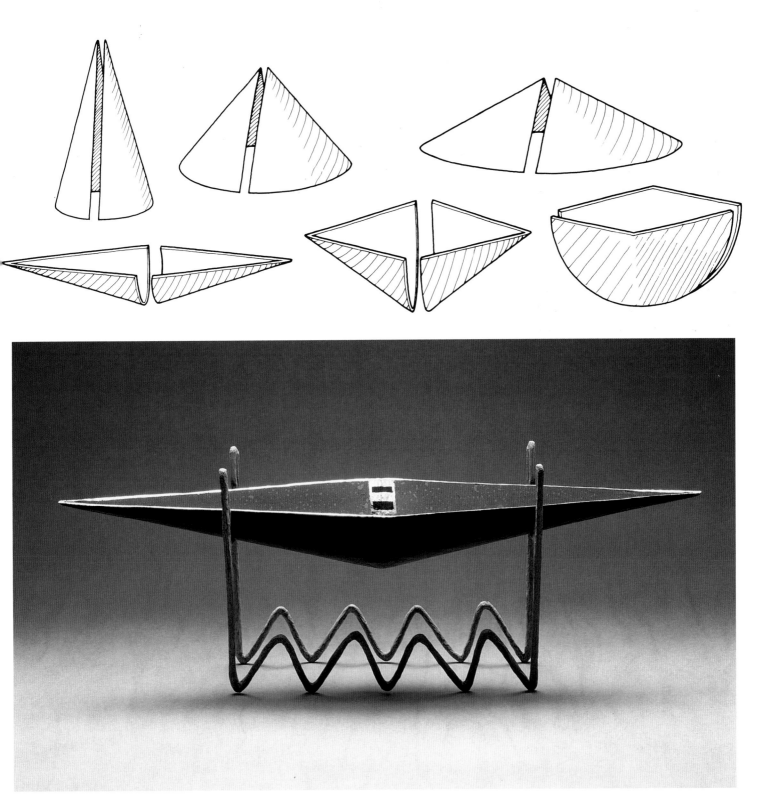

A Double-Cone Bowl

In principle, this bowl is constructed in a similar fashion to the bowl from half cones, but it is made from two entire cones. In addition, the cones are joined together on the diagonal like a miter joint. What results is an unusual, angular form. The container must also be given an opening.

First make two narrow cones, using the layering technique. Model them both on the same working cone so that they turn out the same.

Now cut both cones off at the same angle. To do that, first make an identical cone pattern from a rolled-up sheet of paper and cut it at the desired diagonal angle. To check how it will appear later, place the cone pattern on a mirror. The cut edges are even if they touch the mirror at all points. Now, with the help of the cone pattern, transfer the diagonal angle onto the cone and cut it accordingly. Cut the opening of the container out of the cone pattern as well. Check that it is uniform on the mirror, and cut it out with a sharp knife.

Before assembling the cones, paint the inner surfaces that you will no longer be able to reach afterwards. Apply a carmine red oil glaze to a pink acrylic foundation.

When the paint is dry, put the two halves together. Cover the cut edges with wood glue and join them. Put some tape on the edges so that they stay together during the drying process. Strengthen the outside of the seam with several layers of paper, but not the inside, because it has already been painted. Finally, paste thin brown packing paper over the entire container.

I would call the shade of color of the container a lively, colorful black. Color the brown packing paper with several coats of violet acrylic glaze. The lovely surface re-sults only after it gets a coat of shellac. The pleasant sheen of the shellac enhances the round surfaces of the container.

The base of the container is again a wire frame: several pieces of bent wire joined together and covered with paper mache. The unusual form of the container encourages experimentation. Stands of other shapes would also be possible. The instructions for the wire stands are on page 96. The stand is coated with a red glaze similar to the inside of the container.

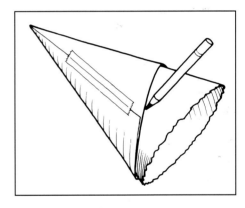

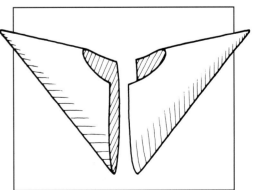

Bowls From Pyramids

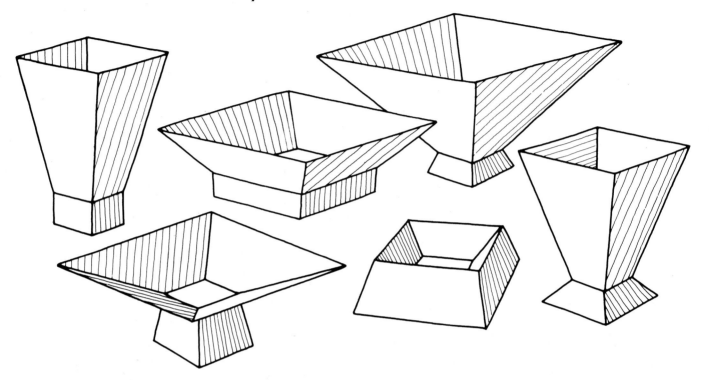

Rectangles are of course among the most common geometric forms, and naturally there are many very interesting possibilities for making objects from rectangular or triangular shapes. Logically, you immediately think of making projects like these out of cardboard, instead of putting forth the effort of building them with paper mache. Angular objects fall more into the category of cardboard work; therefore, I will introduce only a few models with angular shapes.

These three bowls are made from sections of pyramids that were combined in a variety of ways. Cardboard models are needed for all of them. The illustrations show how to go about making them. They are given an additional bottom in order to prevent the sides from buckling. The bowl with the base consists of two single pyra-

mid forms. The cardboard forms must be covered with book wrap so that they do not become damp.

All three bowls are made of pulp. Use only blue handmade paper for the smaller bowl; for the larger one use a mixture of blue and white paper. As a substitute, you may make up a pulp from colored paper napkins.

Divide the pulp into four balls of equal size so that all four sides will be equally strong. Apply these portions to the outer sides and the bottom of the cardboard form. Cover each side of the pyramid bit by bit with pulp. Use your hands to press it on carefully and form a layer equally thick all around, with no gaps. You will need to press along the vertical sides of the form with your thumbs to define the angles.

Then smooth the surfaces with a knife. Finally, smooth out the rim.

The dried paper mache pyramids are easy to release by separating the cardboard model from the bottom while pressing the sides of the model inward. Stronger tension is created in containers with angular sides than in those with round sides because of shrinkage during the drying process. This can cause the sides to bow inward a bit.

For the bowl with the base, glue the two pyramids to the bottom. Finally, polish the edges with sandpaper. Since the paper mache is made from colored materials and not painted, you can apply a coat of wax to protect it from getting dirty without changing the color.

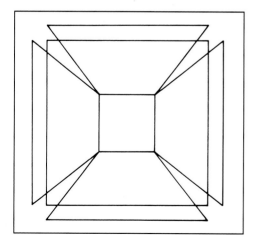
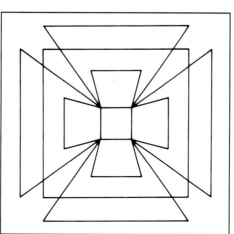
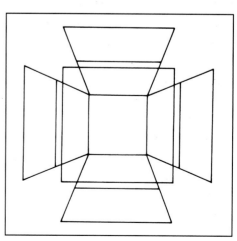

A Pyramid on Legs

This project consists of an upside down pyramid that has no base on which to rest but rather is supported by four legs.

Again, model the pyramid on a supporting framework made of cardboard. Support the working pyramid with a square object on the inside so that it does not get flattened or warped (see illustration). Cover it with book wrap to protect it from moisture.

Place the working pyramid on a platform of suitable size so that it can be rotated easily. No lubricant is necessary. The model shown is made from pulp composed of used white typing paper.

To begin, reserve a small amount of the pulp in the refrigerator for later corrections. Then divide the mass into four large and four small balls. The large balls are for the walls and the small ones for the legs. This way the four sides will be equal.

Now apply the pulp to the working pyramid and work with it as described on the preceding pages. Finally, shape a scalloped rim. To make the pulp more workable for creating the details, add a bit of paste to it. Make the legs separately and glue them on later. In addition, you will need four branch-like pieces, which will become the bones of the "drumsticks." Pad the branches with a thick layer of pulp in the upper areas (see illustration). The points where parts will be attached must be diagonal so that the feet will be at the right angle later on. When the feet are finished, line them up standing next to one another at the points where they will be attached, to check that they are equal in form and angle.

After all the parts are dried, glue the drumsticks on. It is helpful to first mark their positions on the pyramid. Later you will have to sand the bottoms of the feet so they are smooth. Coat them with wood glue and attach them firmly. When the glue is dry, you can cover the seams with little bits of the reserved pulp.

This project model does not require any decoration; it creates an effect through its form and the contrast of the natural materials alone. Objects made of pulp from colored paper can be waxed and polished lightly. Wax results in a nicer, more subtle sheen than clear varnish.

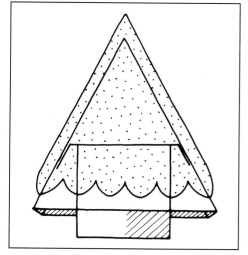

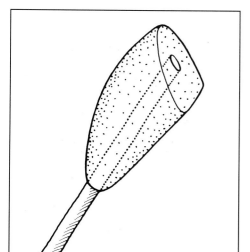

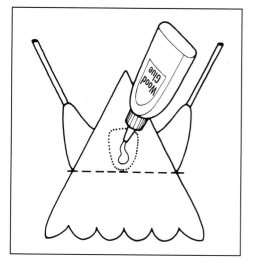

Two Rectangular Baskets

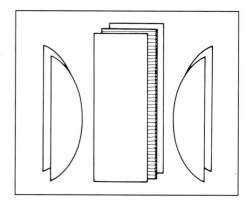

These two baskets have rectangular foundations. Their sides are combined with rounded bottoms.

The green basket is a very simple design. It does not have a firm base, but rather rocks like a cradle on its rounded bottom.

The necessary individual parts are shown in the drawing. The sides are made of double layers of cardboard so that they are strong enough.

The round side sections are cut from corrugated cardboard with the help of a pattern. The curved bottom consists of two layers of flexible cardboard (pasteboard or posterboard) with a padding between them of corrugated cardboard covered with paper strips.

The parts are joined as follows: attach the bottom section to the two sides with wide tape. Then lay the corrugated cardboard and the second bottom section on top. Trim them a bit first so they are a bit narrower. Connect all the layers of the bottom with double-sided tape. Finally, set in the other two side sections. Paste them on firmly with double-sided tape, narrowing them a bit at the top.

Finally, attach narrow strips of cardboard onto the upper edges with tape. That will assure clean contours, and the moisture resulting from pasting on paper strips will not dampen it. That finishes the preliminary construction of the green basket. In order to hide the texture of the corrugated cardboard, first paste a layer of crumpled tissue paper over the entire basket. Follow with two smooth layers. The green basket is decorated using the resist method described on page 187.

The red basket conceals the same construction as the green one, but is surrounded by a case that allows it to stand without moving. All parts are cut from corrugated cardboard; only the bottom is of flexible posterboard (see illustration).

Join together the cardboard surfaces to an inner and an outer form (see illustration). Begin with the outer form and paste it together with tape; apply double layers to the diagonal sides. Then cut the cardboard bottom to the proper width and construct the inner form. Finally, use double-sided tape to join the two parts together. Additional steps are the same as for the green basket.

The red basket has a three-dimensional string decoration, which is described on page 194.

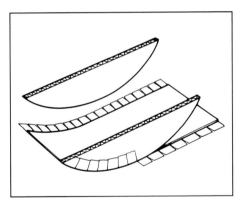

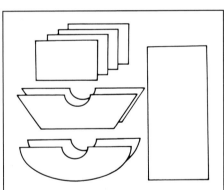

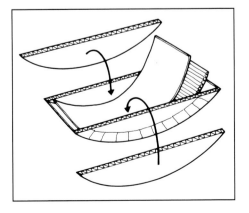

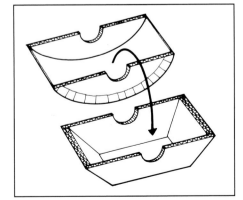

A Diagonal Tray on Two Feet

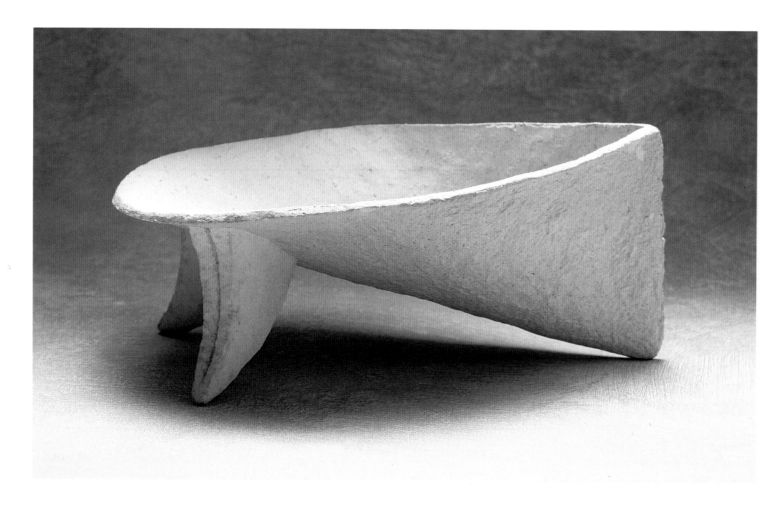

This somewhat unusual tray made of pulp serves as a container for pens and pencils. It resulted from modelling on a supporting structure made of cardboard. Flexible Bristol board, for example, is well suited for the cardboard form. The cardboard piece consists of a rectangle that is cut on a circular line on one side (see illustration).

Cover one side with paint or book wrap to prevent contact with moisture. Measure the center point of the straight edge and fold that edge in half, without bending the rest of the surface. The protective paper is now on the outside. Join the cardboard edges that lie on top of one another with tape and then with paper clips as well (see illustration).

The tray consists of pulp made from used white photocopy paper. You can see the little black specks of toner in the white mass. Before beginning work, reserve a little of the pulp in an air-tight container for later corrections. In addition, reserve about one-fifth of the pulp for the feet.

Now spread the pulp in an even layer onto the outside of the cardboard form and smooth it over with a knife. Create a

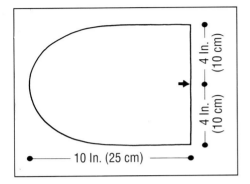

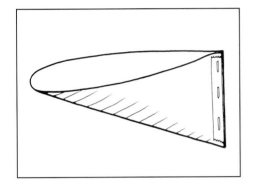

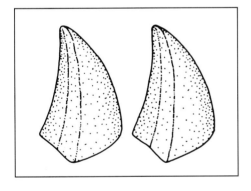

pointed vertical edge at the back and a clean edge at the rim. In the course of the drying process, you can smooth out the surface once again.

Make the feet separately out of the reserved pulp. So that they turn out equal in size, divide the pulp exactly in half before modelling the two feet, which are shaped exactly alike (see illustration). Stand them on end to dry.

The drying process for the pulp can last up to a week. To release the dried paper mache tray, simply bend the supporting construction towards the inside.

If the feet turn out uneven due to shrinkage while drying, you may either sand them or add some of the reserved pulp to make them equal. You may also use sandpaper to smooth the rim of the tray if necessary.

On the tray, mark the desired position of the feet before mounting them. Pay attention to the symmetry! Coat both the surfaces to be joined with white glue and attach the feet. Later you can cover up the joint with bits of pulp so that the tray appears to be all one piece.

Bear Bowl

The bear bowl is one of the few objects that is not made from a solid model but rather from a form of crumpled paper. The advantage of forms made of crumpled paper is that you can create curves that you do not find on everyday objects. Freedom to create different shapes is limited to simple forms, though, which turn out somewhat irregular. Crumpled paper forms such as these are the simplest type of homemade supporting structures.

The shape of the bear bowl is determined by the edge of the cardboard. Draw the desired shape on hard cardboard and cut it out, removing the inside part.

Then attach a relatively large amount of crumpled paper onto the cut-out inner piece of cardboard, which will lend the bowl its curve. Hold the crumpled ball of paper in place on the cardboard with one hand, and wrap yarn around each piece of crumpled paper with the other. Now put the padded cardboard piece back into the opening of the frame and cover both parts equally with pasted strips of paper. Apply the strips of paper lightly so that the padded inner section does not get flattened during the process. Paste strips of paper onto both sides of the cardboard edge. After the paper layer is strong enough and dry, remove the inner cardboard-crumpled-paper section carefully. Cover the inside of the bowl once more with paper strips. You must take care to cover carefully the places where the edges and the rounded areas meet.

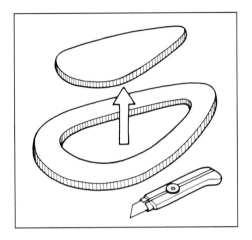

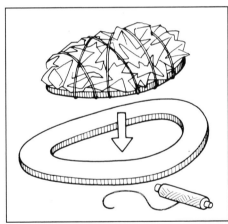

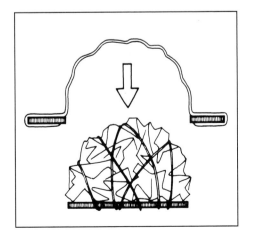

The footprints of bears are beloved motifs in the folk art of North American Indians. To fit that motif, the bear bowl is glazed with brown wood varnish. The bear dance motifs are painted on with a fine brush in indigo-colored acrylic paint.

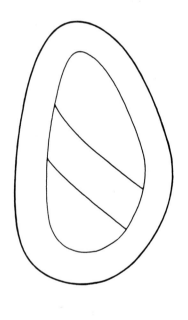

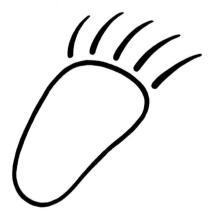

5

Feet

In the three preceding chapters, I introduced a series of bowls that had feet or were supported by a framework. Now I will deal with feet in a special chapter. Bowls can be supported in a variety of ways: on a simple base, by firmly attached feet, or on separate supporting structures. The shape of the support has a great influence on the overall proportions of the container, so feet have a practical as well as a design-related function.

- *Bases*

- *Attached Feet*

- *Cardboard Stands for Cones*

- *Stands in Geometrical Shapes*

- *A Tall Base for Bowls*

- *Wire Supports for Round Containers*

- *Wire Supports for Elongated Containers*

- *The Octopus*

Bases

Many container shapes have no base to support them and therefore need an additional support. In this chapter the various possibilities will be introduced: bases, firmly attached feet, and separate supports in a variety of shapes and designs. In addition to their function as support, feet have a decorative quality as well and can influence the proportions of the container.

Bases in the shape of cones, pyramids, or cylinders are the easiest supports for containers without flat bottoms. The drawings on these pages are meant to illustrate how much the height and breadth of a base influence the entire impression a container makes. The illustrations relate to rounded bowls but can also apply to bowls from cones and pyramids.

Bases from cylinders are the easiest to construct by using available cardboard tubes. If no cardboard tube is available with the desired circumference, then you can use a long strip of cardboard, apply wood glue, and roll it up. Curved bases can be constructed from patterns made from bottles, vases, or cups turned upside down.

Cut the bases at the desired height to fit the bowl. Apply wood glue on the upper edge and attach it to the upended bowl. After the glue is dry, you can paste an additional strip of material onto the inside of the base. If necessary, you can fill in gaps between the base and the bowl with a filler of leftover paper mache pulp.

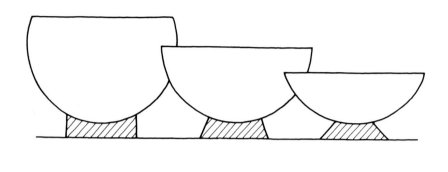

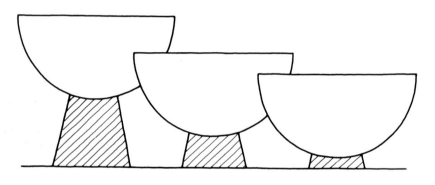

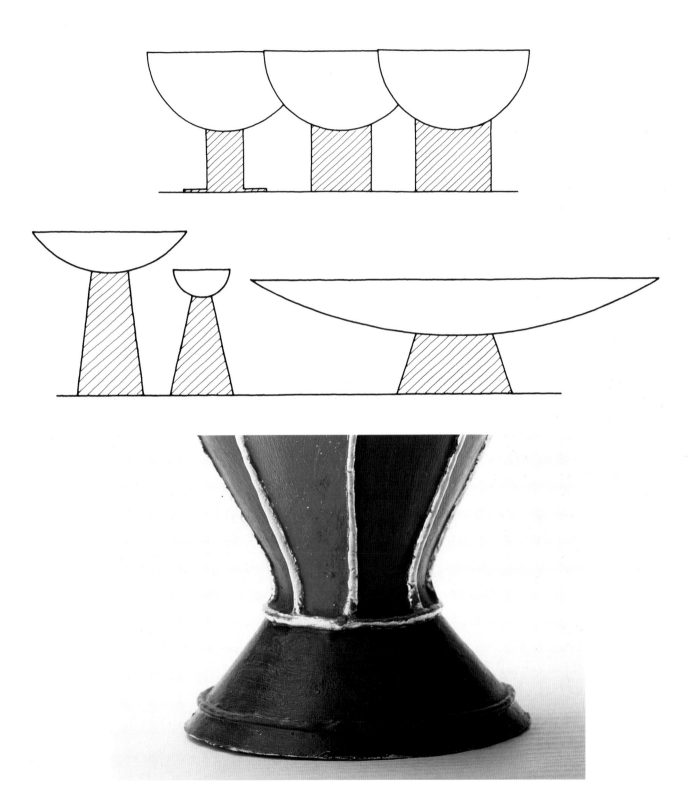

Attached Feet

A base blends nicely with a bowl to create a unified structure and to provide support, but feet are much more obvious because they elevate the bowl.

The variety of possible shapes runs from simple and geometrical to much more elaborate. Use your imagination when shaping the feet. You can lend a simple bowl an unmistakable, decorative character with interesting feet.

There are two different possibilities when making feet. Massive feet are made from pulp separately and glued onto the container after they are dry. They are equally suitable for bowls made of pulp and those using the layering method. As examples of this method, the "drumsticks" on the pyramid container are shown with a description on page 74.

Hollow feet are a part of the paper shell of the container. Make them from plasticine and attach them to the existing container as additions. Then paste paper strips onto the entire form in one process. This is modelling.

The plasticine must be released from the paper shell after it dries. On page 50 there is a detailed description of the steps involved for the Indian motif bowl with seven feet. In many cases, the container must be cut in order to remove the plasticine from the feet. You can learn more about this by reading about the dish with four feet on page 58.

What is true for feet also goes for all other details and decorative elements. They are all basically outgrowths or extensions of the object. They are constructed and attached according to their function.

It is not possible to add decorations made of pulp right onto a piece that is still wet. Nor can you apply fresh pulp onto dried layered paper, because the moisture would cause the background to warp.

No matter whether the feet are made of plasticine or pulp, be careful to make all of them equal in shape and size, and attach them to the container symmetrically. It is best to mark the positions on the piece first. You may cover the seam where the feet have been glued on with very small bits of pulp or with paper strips.

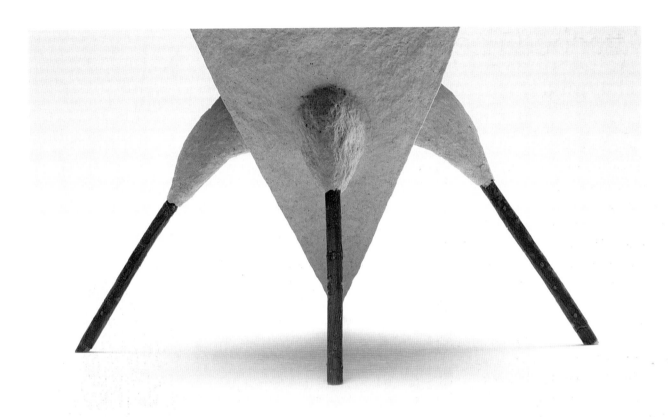

87

Cardboard Stands for Cones

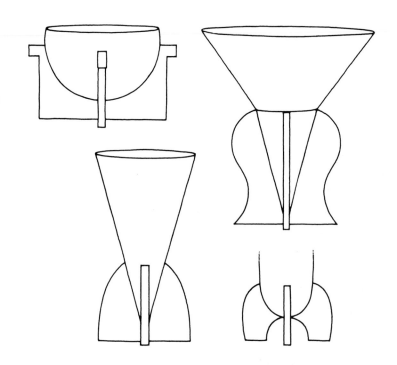

Cone-shaped containers definitely need a support because, unlike spheres, they cannot be balanced on a central point.

The principles of construction shown here apply to separate as well as to attached supports. Stands can consist of three or four vertical supporting points, but even six or more would be possible. As the sketches show, the design can vary—on the outside, depending on the structure of the support, or on the inside, in relation to the container being used.

Constructing a stand like this is simple. Make a pattern of the shape of the stand, then cut it out of cardboard. The object being supported determines the number of elements and how they are connected.

One option is to glue the stand firmly onto the cone. Cut each supporting area out of strong cardboard. Glue the parts onto the cone, and glue the area where the two pieces meet in the middle using strips of bent cardboard. That is how the white bowl was created. Two of the four bases are angled downwards or sideways.

The second possibility is a separate stand. Cut out a double form of corrugated cardboard for each side of the stand and bend each one in the middle. Paste one half onto the next half all the way around (see illustration). The striped stand is constructed this way.

To create a massive appearance, insert two layers of corrugated cardboard in between (again, see illustration). Attach narrow strips of cardboard onto the cut edges of the corrugated cardboard with adhesive tape, so that the edges will be smooth.

Both models are covered with several layers of paper. The white bowl is covered entirely with coarse-grained rice paper.

Paste a layer of crumpled tissue paper onto the separate stand in order to cover the corrugated cardboard. The crinkled texture is brought out again in the striped pattern. Gild the vertical edges. Further details about decorating techniques are found on page 188 and 196.

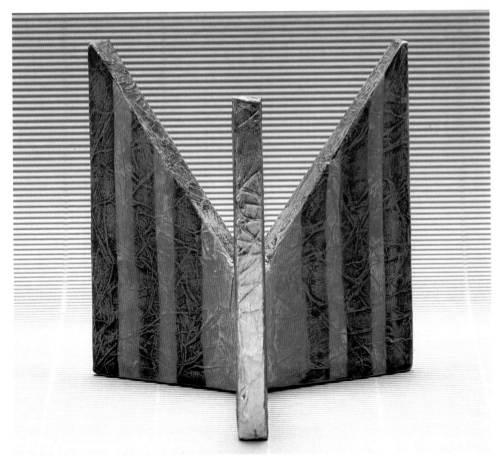

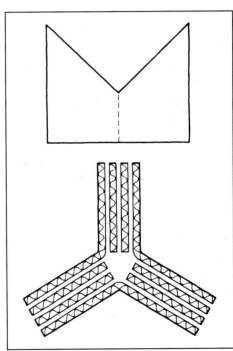

Stands Made From Geometric Shapes

What follow are two additional separate stands, which fit a variety of shapes of bowls. These models appear massive but are actually hollow. But they do need to be combined with rather large bowls because of their optical effect, so that the proportions are balanced.

The black stand is made from three equal narrow cones. The cones must be stable, so that the stand can do its job. They consist of about 20 paper layers; in addition, the tips are filled out with left-over pulp.

All three cones must be cut at the same angle. To facilitate this, make a cone pattern from a piece of paper that has been rolled up and cut at the desired angle. The cut edge is straight if it touches a surface evenly all the way around. Now draw the angle on the three cones with the help of the upended cone pattern and cut along the lines with a knife.

Then paste the three cones onto a base of cardboard. In order to make it easier to arrange them in the right positions, divide the cardboard base into six parts onto which you mark the ovals formed by the cut surfaces of the cone. The cones can be arranged with the help of these marks. Glue the cones to the base. After the glue is thoroughly dry, cut away the extra cardboard with a sharp knife. Glue strips of paper onto the seams. Paint the stand black and coat it with shellac.

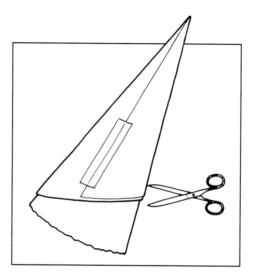

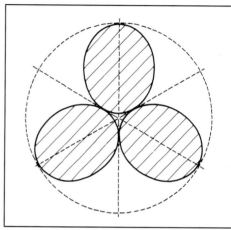

The yellow stand resembles the ruins of a small Roman temple. First make a ring-shaped cardboard base. To do that, paste three or four rings of corrugated cardboard on top of one another and enclose them on the outside with a narrow rim of cardboard.

The pillars are cut from cardboard rolls. Each pillar ends in a cone shape. Make six little temporary cones from heavy paper. Fill them with leftover pulp

to make them stable. Then turn them upside down onto the pillars. After the pulp is dry, either remove the temporary paper cones or cut them down to fit.

Paste layers of paper over all the parts, the pillars and the round base. Finally, glue the pillars onto the base equidistant apart. Prime the yellow stand with gesso and apply a glaze of oil paint in a light ocher color.

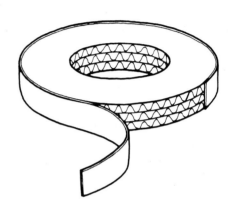

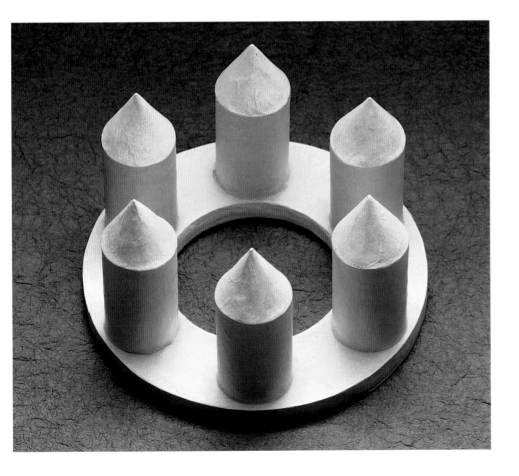

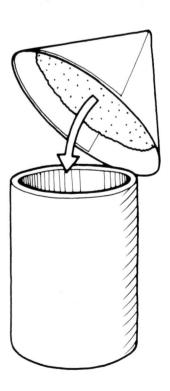

A Pedestal for Bowls

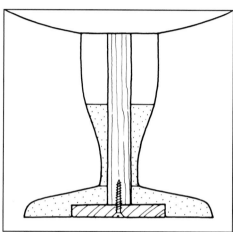

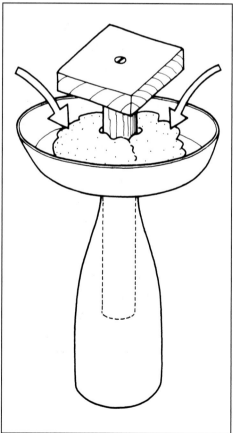

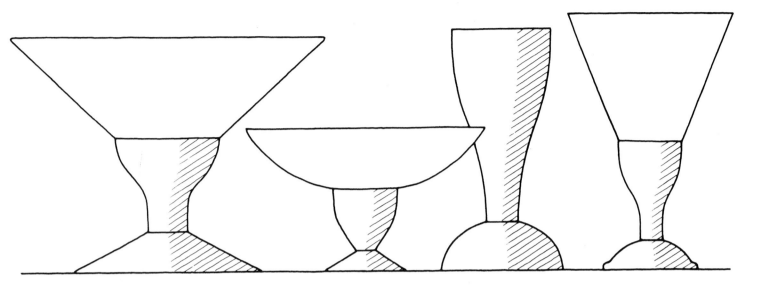

This tall base is meant to support large, flat bowls. You can either make a corresponding bowl for it and attach it firmly, or use it as a separate stand for bowls already on hand.

The base is modelled with layered paper on a bottle and a pot lid. Possible variations result from the choice of bottle, a vase (for example, flat cones or sphere patterns), and the bowl that is being used.

When modelling the lid, leave the handle area open. After the bottle is covered with paper and allowed to dry, cut the paper form off the bottle and glue the cut edges together again. Arrange the two paper shells to test the effect, and decide how much of the bottle needs to be cut off at the top and the bottom. Glue the two shells together. Later, round out the glued joint with leftover pulp.

The base has to be stabilized so that the large bowl does not tip it. To do that, first cut a small square of wood and screw a piece of a broomstick to the middle. Turn the paper shell upside down onto it, measure the proper height, and saw off the broomstick so that it fits. If the base of the bowl extends into the bottle, the broomstick will have to be cut down to leave more room.

Paint the inside of the paper shell to protect it. Turn the pedestal upside down, fill the base with some thick plaster of Paris, and press the wooden support in as far as possible so that the little board closes off at the rim.

Then turn the whole thing back up again to dry. Check that the base is standing truly vertical. After the plaster of Paris hardens, it forms a stable link between the inside and the paper form, in addition to adding necessary weight.

Now you can fill the rest of the pedestal with plaster of Paris. Stuff crumpled paper covered with paste into the top of the pedestal so that a smooth surface results. In this way the bowl has a good supporting surface.

If the bowl is to be permanently attached to the base, use wood glue to do so. In addition, you can put a roofing nail into the broomstick through the base of the bowl.

The base has a terra cotta–colored pattern on a blue gesso foundation. It is a special type of inlay work. Further information is found on page 189.

Wire Frames for Round Containers

Wire frames offer a variety of possibilities for supporting containers that don't have built-in bases. In addition, wire frames can be used for candle holders, lamp shades, and hanging devices.

The decorative stand is covered with paper mache and creates the effect of wrought iron. Its linear shape creates a contrast to the flat form of the container. There is no limit to the shapes that can be used, apart from their structural requirements.

All supports shown were made by bending 12 gauge (2 mm) zinc-coated steel wire. This gauge provides good stability, but it can still be cut and bent without any problem. You will need wire cutters, flat-edged pincers, and round-nosed pliers (for bending the wire). For joining parts together, use thin floral wire.

The stands are assembled from several parts made of bent wire. This method of construction is the same for all round stands, with certain variations.

To make it easier, draw the desired circumference of the stand on a piece of paper. Using this drawing, measure the length of wire needed for one foot. One foot equals two of the vertical legs plus a quarter of the circumference of the base (see illustration). Cut the wire pieces accordingly and mark the measurements on them, so you'll know where to bend them later.

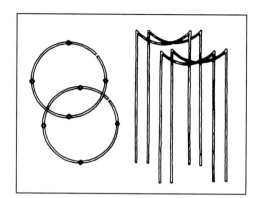

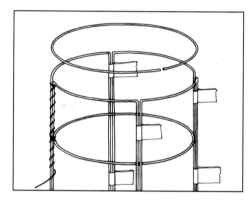

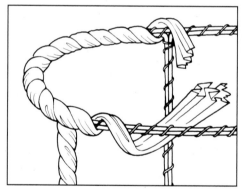

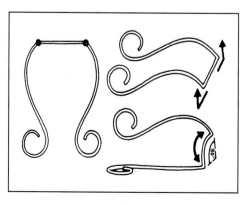

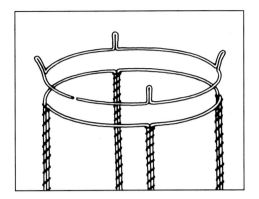

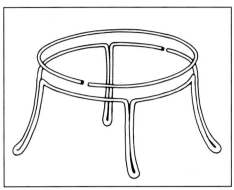

Now assemble the stand. Bend each section of wire in two places, to form the vertical legs. Join the four large feet together to form a circle (see illustration). Two parallel wires form each leg. Attach them temporarily with adhesive tape.

Cut a piece of wire to fit around the circumference of the circle, and join it to the middle part of the foot, following the illustration. Some models require a second ring between the feet. It prevents the feet from spreading apart under the weight they support. Now the entire stand is made of double wire. Wrap thin floral wire all around it (see illustration).

If the feet are to be curved, you will have to determine the curve in a drawing. Using the drawing, bend the feet while they are lying flat. Then bend them forward, away from the middle center, at a right angle. Finally, bend the middle part into a round shape (see illustration).

When the stand is finished, cover it with a layer of paper mache about $1/8$ inch (3 mm) thick. To do that, cut a strip of tissue paper about 2 inches (5 cm) wide, gather it together lengthwise, and wrap it around all the wire parts (see illustration). Then wrap the base one to three more times to reach desired thickness.

Since the basic technique is always the same, I have simply illustrated the construction of additional wire frames with drawings of their component parts.

Wire Stands for Elongated Containers

The wire stands shown here are created exactly as described on earlier pages. They are also made from many sections of bent wire, which are bound together with thin floral wire and covered with paper mache. The only difference is in their shape.

Although the stands for the two bowls made from half cones on page 68 have different proportions, they are constructed according to the same principle. But they are also suitable for supporting other elongated containers.

Both frames have four vertical supports, which are joined by two bases below and two half arches set on top. The containers hang in the semicircular arches between the two vertical buttresses.

The lower connecting piece, which forms the base, runs straight along the base of the stand at top right of page 97; the stand below, is made to appear looser by a zigzag line. The shape of the arch must fit the curves of the corresponding container.

From the illustrations you can see how the wire sections of these two models are formed. It is also advisable to make a sketch showing how the wires should be bent for these stands.

The red wire frame was created for the double-cone container on page 70. The unusual form of the container encourages some experimentation and results in a custom-tailored frame.

Two arches surround and hold the body of the container. The two arches are joined together at their tips and are supported by feet. The tips must be bent apart briefly when setting in the container, because the curves get narrower at the top.

Here as well, the method of construction is perhaps clearer in the illustration than through any number of words.

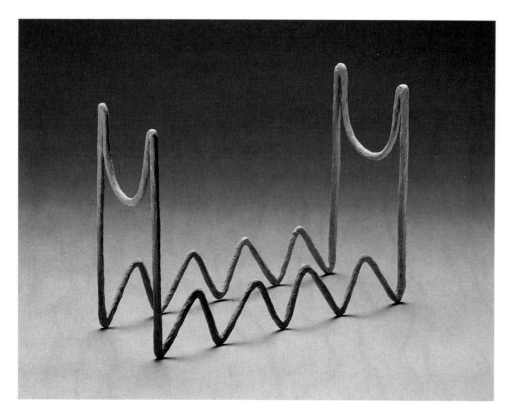

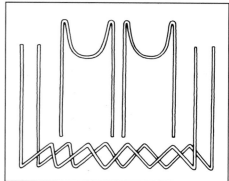

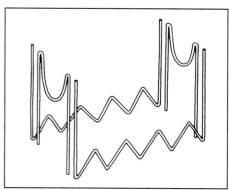

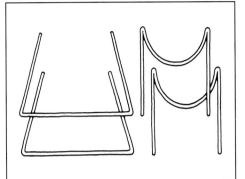

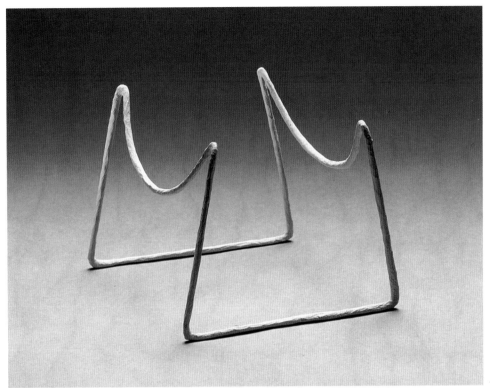

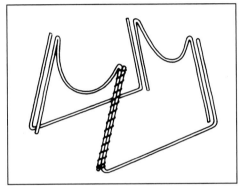

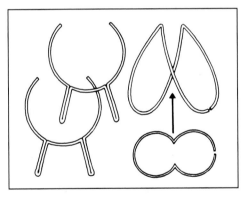

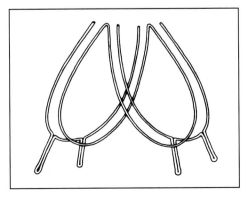

The Octopus

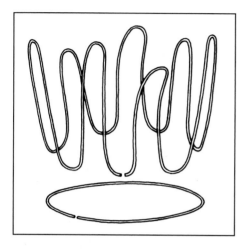

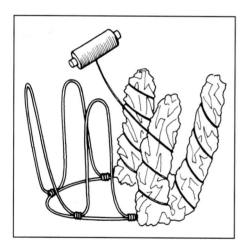

This stand is also basically a wire frame; its skeleton, however, is hidden inside. It is an example of the additional possibilities when using wire constructions. By thick padding with crumpled paper, it gives the impression of a massive body.

The many arms of the stand give it the name Octopus. It can be used with the arms facing up or facing down. Although the arms are irregularly shaped, four of them have the same height, so that even when they are upside down, they create a firm base.

If the octopus is standing upright, it is suitable for a cone-shaped bowl; if it is standing upside down, it looks best with a very large flat bowl. But in any case, its massive appearance requires a strong counterweight so that the proportions are balanced.

First, bend some wire into a ring shape, which determines the circumference of the stand. Then bend an additional piece of wire to form the arms reaching upwards all around (see illustration). Bend them slightly outward and do not let them look too uniform. Bind together the row of arms and the ring with thin wire.

Turn the wire framework upside down and bend each of the arms into place where necessary, so that it stands upright without wobbling. To test this, place a glass of water on it.

Finally, pad the frame with crumpled newspaper. Wrap it with yarn to hold it together temporarily. Then cover the arms of the octopus with strips of tissue paper soaked in paste. Be especially careful when pasting paper on areas between the arms forming a circle. After applying about six layers, allow the object to dry.

After the paper layer is dry, it is easy to correct any small mistakes. Any disturbing bulges, bumps, or edges can be smoothed out with a rasp or even cut off. Indentations can be padded with a bit of crumpled paper covered with a little paste or filled in with leftover pulp. After making these corrections, cover the entire frame with six additional layers of paper.

The octopus has a black primer onto which a mosaic of torn strips of paper is pasted. In addition, its arms are decorated with red and white strips of paper. The mosaic pattern is a little reminiscent of the broken pieces of tile used by the Spanish architect Gaudi. A charming contrast results between the fluid shapes and the stony hardness suggested by the mosaic.

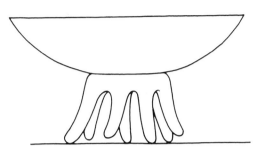

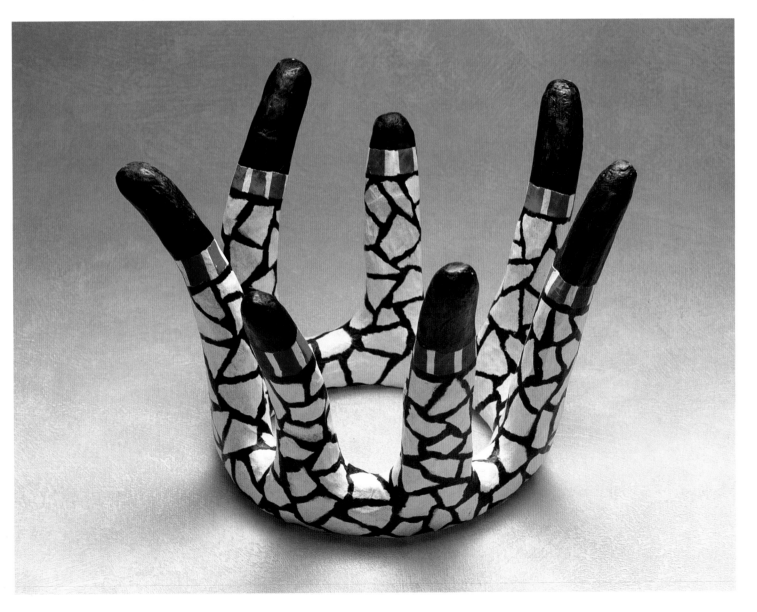

6

Containers With Lids

This chapter deals with boxes, cans, and cases that can be closed, with directions for making both classic closures and experimental ones.

- *Classic Closures*
- *Stacking Cans*
- *Cone Case*
- *Experimental Clasps From Sticks*
- *Cases With Hinged Lids*
- *Mummy Case and Folding Case*
- *Pod Case*

Classic Closures

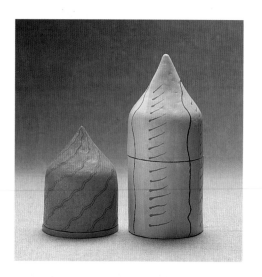

If you wander around your house and look carefully, you will run across cans, boxes, tea canisters, and cooking pots with an array of classic lids. The greatest difficulty with lids is the little bit of "air" they require—the careful fit between the container and the lid, because a lid must fit neither too tightly nor too loosely.

It is challenging to think up a way of making the intended type of closure from paper mache as accurately as possible. It is important to include shrinkage from drying in your calculations.

The lid of the tall, green can covers less than half of the bottom part. It is supported by a narrow rim. To create the necessary fit, the sides of the lid are thinner than those of the lower section.

The lower section is a narrow tin can (a lost form) covered with pulp. The upper rim of the can remains free of pulp; cover it with strips of masking tape. Cover the can with pulp up to the level of the tape (see illustration). The rim of the pulp must be shaped very carefully to form a horizontal ledge.

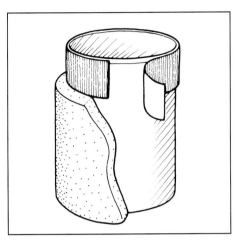

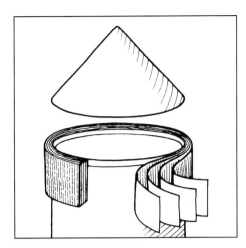

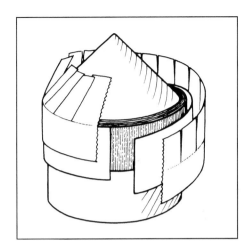

A second tin can is needed for the lid. Paste four layers of masking tape around the lower rim (see illustration). Then apply a layer of thin cardboard. Keep in mind that the lid must sit loosely enough so that it can be turned. Place a temporary cardboard cone on the bottom of the can. Join the cone and strips of cardboard with broad strips of waterproof12 tape and cover the entire object with tape to protect it (see illustration}. These different layers allow the lid to fit loosely later on.

The lid must be turned around frequently during the drying process so that it remains loose. Only when it is entirely dry

can it be removed. Then the cardboard layer can be removed.

The lid of the small red can comes down almost completely over the bottom half of the can; only the flat base remains visible. The base allows you to get a grip on the lower half in order to open it. Two identical cans are needed for this project.

Coat the sides of the first tin can with lubricant and place a piece of aluminum foil cut to fit onto the bottom. Then cover the inside with a layer of pulp. That forms the bottom half.

The bottom half will shrink inside the tin can and will be easy to remove. Set this

bottom half on a flat, round surface made of pulp which extends out about $1/2$ inch (1 cm) beyond the edge. The base is formed in this way.

The lid is formed from the second can. Attach a cardboard cone onto the bottom. Cover the outside of the entire piece, which becomes a lost form, with pulp. Shape the transition between the can and the cone to form a rounded curve.

When the can is dry, sand the paper mache surfaces. Smooth out the edges especially carefully with a file or a sharp knife. Finally, paste tissue paper on the inside of the cans.

Both cans were given several coats of primer, polished, then given a coat of color. The thin lines of the pattern were applied with a small bottle of latex gutta.

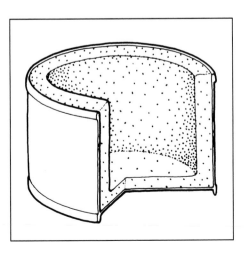

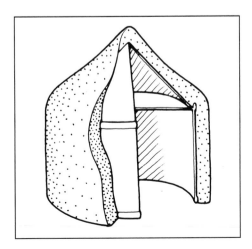

Stacking Cans

The stacking can is another container with a classic closure. Under the lid, as well as under every can, you will find a small base ring of paper mache, which extends down into the can below and holds the two together. All four cans have two winged decorations, which can be used as handles. Depending on how you turn the can, the wings form a regular or an irregular pattern.

You will need four tin cans, which will be covered with pulp and be used as lost forms. The pulp is made of white typing paper with sawdust added (the recipe is on page 21). It is advisable to divide the pulp into equal parts for the cans, the wings, and the lid beforehand, so that they turn out the same thickness and size. Cover all four cans with pulp. Allow it to extend about $1/8$ inch (3 mm) beyond the edge of the can to allow for shrinkage. Cover the pulp with some paste and, using two fingers, form a neat edge; smooth out the surface with a knife. Then allow the cans to dry.

In the meantime, you can make the lid. To do that, make a small, very flat working cone of heavy cardboard and cover it with lubricant. Then model the lid with pulp. Like the cans, the lid must also be made a little too large, because it will shrink when it dries.

After the pieces are thoroughly dry, smooth out the surface with a file. Use a piece of sandpaper to smooth around the edges of the cans. File the edge of the lid so that it fits exactly.

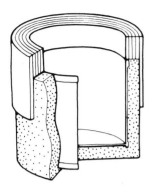

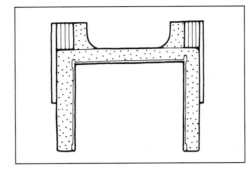

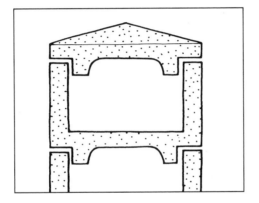

The next step is to make the base ring under the lid and on the bottom of the cans. Make a pattern template for that (see illustration). To do that, wrap a broad strip of cardboard around one of the finished cans and paste it together. Push the cardboard up above the upper rim of the can; how high you push it determines the height of the base. Now paste more narrow strips of cardboard around the inside of the cardboard ring, until it fits the inside of the can exactly.

Move the template to the bottom of the can. Coat the bottom of the can with glue and work a ring of pulp inside the template. Then carefully remove the template. Work in the same way with the lid. Polish the underside of the base after it is dry.

Model the wings separately and glue them onto the cans while they are still fresh. The two wing shapes are the same, but they are attached in opposite directions. They must be positioned exactly opposite one another and be lined up straight.

Paste a layer of tissue paper over the inside of the cans, or coat them with a mixture of paper mache and glue; then paint them dark blue.

Cone Case

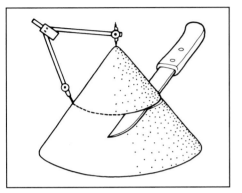

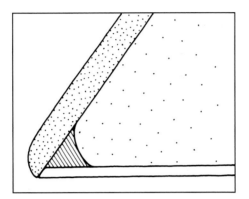

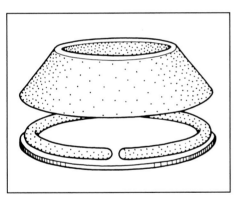

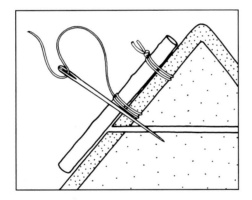

After demonstrating how to make classic closures, I would like to introduce several experimental ones. There are many ways to prevent a lid from falling off, and in addition to cans and boxes, there are many types of containers that can be closed. Closings that you invent yourself can function surprisingly simply and are usually equally simple to make. For example, with the help of a small stick, you can develop the most varied, playful closures. The lid of the cone case shown here is held together with sticks, which are wider than the bottom of the container.

To make the case, first make a cone from pulp (see page 62). Shape the bottom edge into a curve. The pulp in the models shown gets a livelier texture from added sawdust. Reserve a small portion of the pulp for later steps.

When the cone is dry, check with a compass whether the bottom edge is uniform. If necessary, cut it so it is correct and polish it.

Now draw the dividing line for the lid opening with a compass. If it is too low, the case will have too small a capacity; if it is too high, the opening will be too narrow

for you to reach inside. Cut the cone horizontally into two parts with a long, sharp kitchen knife.

Cut a base out of heavy cardboard to fit into the bottom of the case. Coat both the edge of the base and the inside edge of the cone with wood glue about $3/4$ inch (2 cm) thick. Create a thick lip around the edge of the base with the reserved pulp and place the cone on top of it. Join the two parts with tape. Then run your finger along the joint on the inside, mashing the pulp into the joint, so that the two sides are joined.

Eight twigs of equal size and strength are needed for the clasp. Cut them to equal length and cut notches into them where you intend to sew them to the case. In addition, pull off the bark from some of the areas as decoration.

The illustration shows the position of the sticks. Punch out holes with an awl. (A strong needle can be used instead.) Then sew the eight twigs to each of the two points with two colors of yarn. To finish, knot the ends of the yarn.

Experimental Clasps From Sticks

These two containers are also outfitted with closures made from sticks. Apart from their practical function, the sticks lend the containers an exotic flair.

The rounded container is made from three parts: a sphere, a piece of a cardboard tube, and a flat base. For the rounded body, cover a balloon with paper and cut it off at the desired height. With a large, sharp kitchen knife, cut a piece from a cardboard tube to fit. Mark the position of the cardboard ring on the round body and cut out the opening to fit, using a craft knife. Then glue on the tube piece. After that, paste the entire object onto the base. Cut off the excess base with a sharp knife. Finally, paste several layers of paper over the entire container, including the inside of the neck and the bottom of the base.

Construct the lid from a narrow ring of the same cardboard tube. Fill it out with several layers of cardboard and cover it with tissue paper.

After you paint the container, attach the twigs for the closure. The closure consists of small sticks or bamboo chopsticks, which are sewn sideways onto the neck and the lid with embroidery yarn. The vertical sticks at the neck are positioned between the two horizontal ones on the lid. A handle is attached between the two sticks on the lid. It is made of a wire loop wrapped tightly with yarn.

The box, like all objects consisting of straight surfaces, is a borderline case be-

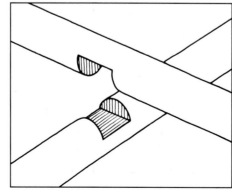

tween cardboard work and paper mache. For the bottom half, make a small, square box from heavy corrugated cardboard. Attach the individual parts with sturdy tape. To strengthen the sides, add one or two additional layers of corrugated cardboard on the inside. Bind together the cardboard layers with double-sided tape. You can also use a finished cardboard box, if it is

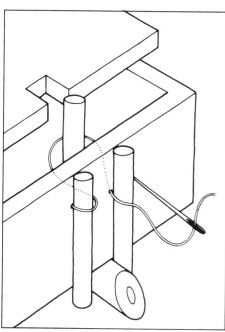

available, and strengthen it on the inside with additional layers of corrugated cardboard.

The flat, square lid fits the outer dimensions of the bottom half. The thickness of the material is equal too. Cut narrow openings for the sticks used as holders in the center of each side.

Cover both the box and the lid with several layers of paper. Crumple the first layer to make the texture livelier. Decorate the piece before adding the sticks for the closing mechanism.

Make a cross of medium-sized twigs and attach them to the underside of the box. Cut a notch into the area where these two pieces of wood cross each other, tie them with yarn, and sew them firmly to the bottom. The cross under the bottom and the little sticks on the outside of the box are purely for decoration. The lid is held only by the sticks on the inside of the box. They extend into the openings in the lid and hold it firmly. The little sticks are notched on top and underneath and sewn together firmly with embroidery yarn (see illustration).

Both containers are decorated with a striped pattern—the little box with indigo on white, the rounded vessel with dark brown on light beige. Some sections of the box have an additional brown-yellow glaze. The severe contrast of the striped pattern is relieved by a patina—for the box, a very diluted yellowish color, and for the rounded can, a thin layer of gesso (see also page 198).

Finally, polish both objects with wax. As you do that, rub some of the underlying layers of colors partly away, so that a livelier texture results.

Cases With Hinged Lids

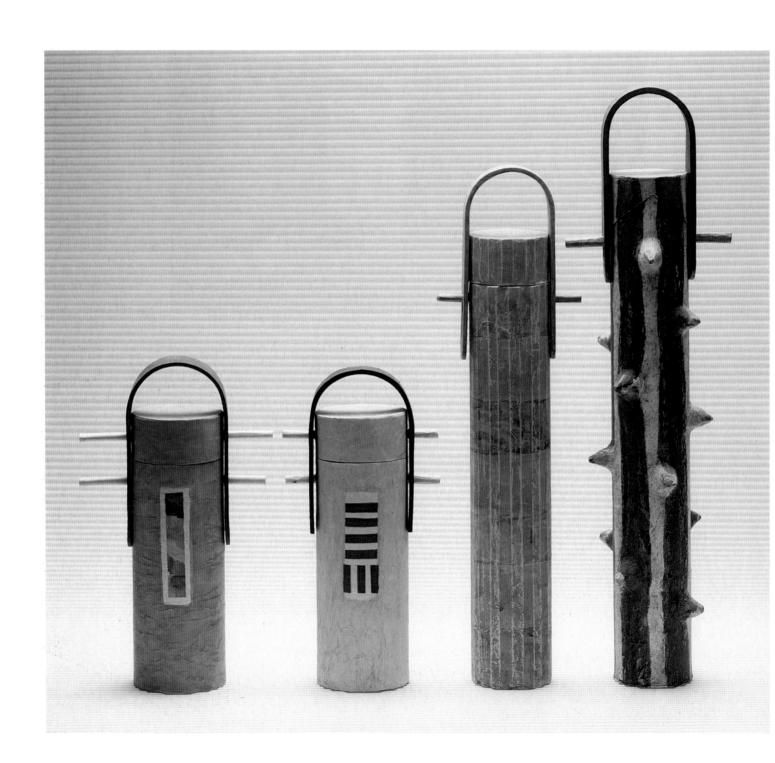

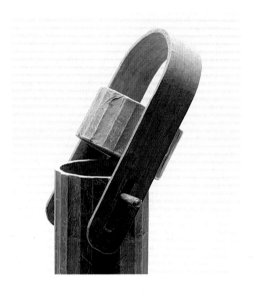

These cases for brushes or rolled drawings are quick and easy to make from readily available cardboard tubes. The unusual touch is the strap, and it takes some patience to construct. The strap is firmly attached to the lid. To open the case, you lift the lid and push it to the side.

Use a cardboard tube in the desired length for the case and a short piece for the lid. Use a large, sharp kitchen knife to cut the tube. Each section has either a top or a bottom made of cardboard. To make the case look nicer, strips of cardboard or small cones of pulp can be pasted to the tube. Then paste several layers of tissue paper onto this rough form. The various materials are joined into an organic unity by the paper shell.

The strap is not bent but rather laminated into shape like layers of wood. Cut about 10 strips of flexible cardboard. Using wood glue, attach them layer by layer around the curve of the same cardboard tube used for the case (see illustration). Take care during the drying process that the horseshoe form is correctly shaped, not just at the curve but also in the straight parts. Allow the strap to harden an entire day before working on it any further. Then, with a sharp knife, cut the sides so they are very smooth and round off the edges (see illustration). Finally, cut the slit in the strap. Punch out the end points with a punch and cut out the middle piece (see illustration).

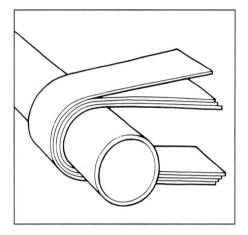

The bottom half has sticks to support the strap. Push two nails with large, flat heads through the tube from the inside and attach them firmly with paste. Working from the outside, stick a little roll of paper or a small, hollow stick over the nail and paste it on firmly. For short cases to carry pencils, just push a little wooden stick through diagonally and fasten it with some adhesive. The lid is either glued to the strap or joined by sticking a chopstick through both the lid and the strap. First paint the pieces, then assemble them.

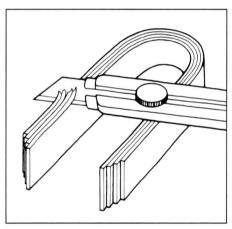

Both the case and the strap are painted with one color of acrylic paint or have simple patterns painted on. The scratched-looking texture results from light sketching with chalk pastels (see page 189).

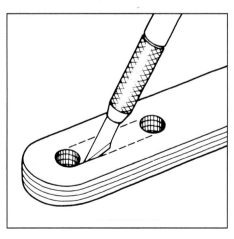

Mummy Case and Folding Case

The two cases on these pages may function differently, but they are related in their basic form. Both cases consist of two oblong halves, which fit together like two halves of a cut loaf of bread. The mummy is a case that can be used vertically; its head is a removable lid. The blue folding case consists of two equal, horizontal halves which are tied together with elastic cord and which can be opened up.

The basic shape for both cases is made from a clay model, which has an oblong shape. Allow the model to dry for two days, as it should not shrink any more.

The clay model for the mummy must be covered with paper two times, one after the other. Cover the form with aluminum foil before pasting the paper on it. Press the foil tightly around the form. It protects the clay model from moisture and serves as a releasing agent at the same time. Put two strips of plastic wrap on top to make it easier to remove the clay model later (see illustration). Lay the form flat on a board and paste on paper strips. Allow the paper to extend about $1/8$ inch (a couple of millimeters) beyond the base.

With the help of the clay model, draw the flat ring that encircles the mummy on heavy cardboard and cut it out. Join the finished halves by pasting them to both sides of the cardboard ring (see illustration). Cover uneven parts with leftover paper mache, and, finally, glue white tissue paper over the entire mummy.

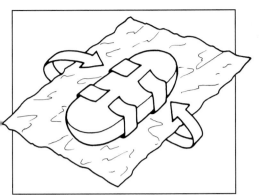
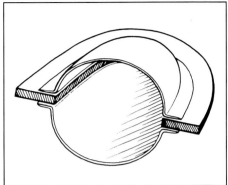
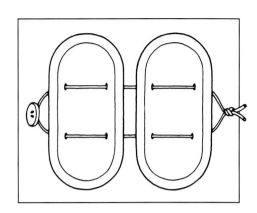

Now the case can be cut horizontally. In order for the mummy to be able to close, set a cardboard ring into the bottom half. It consists of four layers of cardboard. The first two layers end at the rim and assure that the lid has air. Paste the next two layers on so that they extend out over the top of the bottom half and hold the lid.

The face of the mummy is painted with dark blue lines and filled in with a shiny, colored glaze. Coat the object with a dull clear finish to protect it.

The folding case must be made from pulp because the edges of the two halves must be broad enough to be able to fold down onto one another. If the case were made with the layering technique, the narrow edges would slide apart.

Apply two layers of pulp around the clay model to make a casting. If you wish to avoid a long wait for the object to dry, make a second, identical clay model so that both halves of the case can be made at the same time. Polish the two finished halves till smooth. The edges must be polished smooth with special care so that they fit tightly when closed. To do that, lay a piece of sandpaper down and rub the edges of each half in circles on it. Then punch out holes for the elastic cord with a punch. Do this from the outside so that no impressions are left on the bottom half.

Prime the outside of the folding case with several coats of gesso and continue to sand it each time. That is how the raw paper mache takes on a smooth surface. Then apply a glaze of blue oil paint to the outside and the edges. Finally, thread a strong elastic cord through the punched holes and tie the ends in knots (see illustration). This replaces the hinge. At the same time, the cords on the inside also form a support for writing utensils or the like.

Sew a nice button onto the cord, so that you can close the case.

Pod Case

If you look around in nature for containers, you will come across seedpods (as well as cocoons, snail shells, and seashells). This case is inspired by the shape of just such a pod.

The slightly bent, rounded shape is formed from a large clump of crushed newspaper. The ball of paper is pressed into a form, roughed up, and then tied up with thread; this holds its shape (see illustration). The form is rounded on one side; the opposite side has to be straight because of the hinge.

Paste long strips of tissue paper around the ball of tied-up paper. Lay the paper strips on carefully and smooth them only lightly. Apply only light pressure where the sections bulge out too much to make the strips of paper smooth. After five layers have been applied, the pod must dry so that the upper surface becomes firm. If you continue pasting strips of paper on now, it is best to smooth them down firmly but without pressing in on the form. The finished pod must be stable enough so that it will not buckle.

When the pod is dry, cut it lengthwise into two halves. By measuring and estimating, determine the middle line, mark it, and cut along it with a craft knife. If you cut through the inside of the pod with a long kitchen knife, you will find an interesting creased texture, and it is almost a shame to destroy it. But because the pod is to serve as a container, the paper ball must be removed.

Now join together the two edges of the pod halves. Coat the front, curved, cut edges with a good amount of wood glue and place them on a piece of heavy cardboard, so that the cardboard closes in the back but extends beyond the form at the front and side (see illustration). Mark the width of the edge of one half and cut it off; then add it to the other half. The inside surface of the cardboard can be carefully cut away only after the glue has dried (see illustration). Round out the area between the edge and the curve of the pod with pulp or putty. Finally, paste a layer of tissue paper over the entire pod, inside and out.

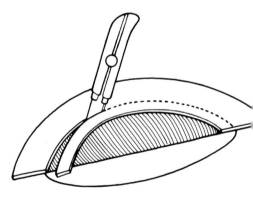

The hinge of the pod consists of a strip of leather, which is glued in. It becomes invisible between the layers of the paper. Carefully separate the cut edges along the back with a knife and split open the shell of paper about 3/4 inch (2 cm) (see illustration). Paint the pod, then glue the leather strips into both sides of the divided area, which has been prepared.

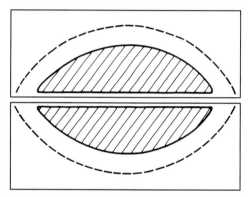

Apply a coat of white primer on the inside and rub in rose pink oil paint. Coat the outside with several layers of glaze, alternating red and black. Then apply a coat of shellac. The hairy inside of the pod consists of red sisal. Thread short pieces of sisal cord through the paper shell and tie them inside. Finally, twist the ends of the cord.

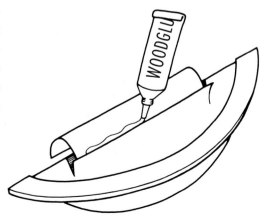

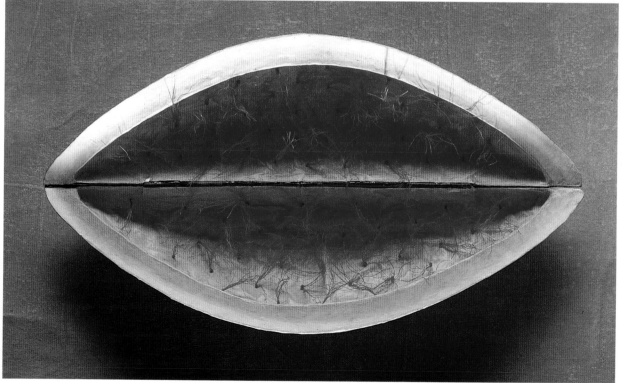

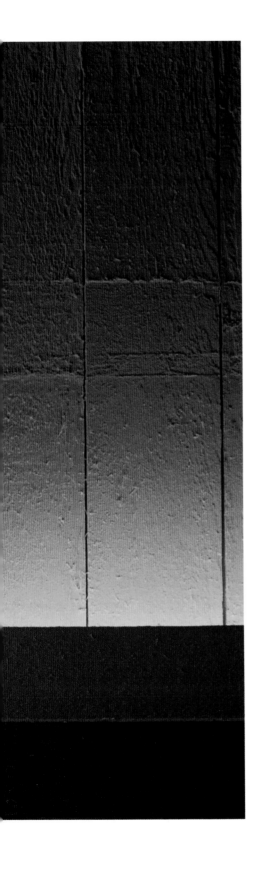

7

Decorations for the Home

This chapter will introduce a variety of objects that can serve as decorative elements for the home. Of course, other paper mache items enhance home decor as well, but these are designed to take their place, like furniture, among home furnishings. Two-dimensional ornaments, as well as picture and mirror frames, decorate the walls of a home. Lanterns and lamps add beautiful light to a seating area.

- *A Wall Relief*

- *Rosette for the Door*

- *Plaster of Paris Wall Decorations*

- *Two Suns*

- *Flat Picture Frames*

- *Decorative Frame for a Mirror*

- *Sun Mirror*

- *Swiveling Mirror on a Stand*

- *Lanterns on Wire Frames*

- *Four-Footed Lamps*

- *A Green Lamp*

- *Lamps with Pointed Shades*

A Wall Relief

On the following pages several varied, three-dimensional objects will be introduced, which are meant as wall decorations and which are made using a variety of techniques.

This pair of decorations is made from one basic three-dimensional form. They have the shape of stylized fruit or buds, and their surfaces are covered with lavish, vivid decoration. This lends a floral character to a simple basic form and is a little reminiscent of Turkish faience.

Many container shapes, such as vases or urns, would also be suitable for cutting in half to make wall reliefs. A pair of decorations made that way could frame a doorway or window very stylishly.

The paper shell—a bottle shape joined to a cone shape—is made with the layering technique. It closely resembles the amphora on page 53, but it is upside down.

Cover a rounded wine bottle or vase with paper layers. Cut the shell away from the form along one side, and then glue it back together again. Now glue a tall, narrow cone onto the bottle-shaped shell. Sand the seam until smooth and paste strips of paper over it.

Cut the finished shell lengthwise into two equal halves. To add strength, attach a back wall of corrugated cardboard to each half. (For better stability, cut the cardboard so that the ribs are diagonal.) To do that, trace around the object on cardboard and cut it out. Coat the cut edges with glue and place the cardboard between the outside

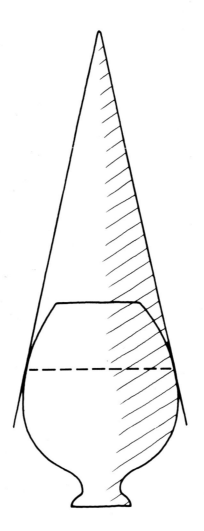

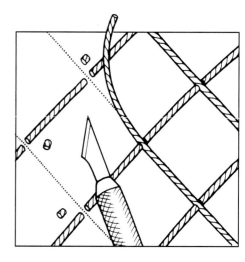

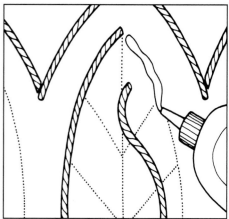

back walls. Punch a hole into the upper part of the back for hanging.

The three-dimensional decoration consists of pieces of string pasted onto the surface. First draw the pattern on the paper shell with a pencil and then, using wood glue, glue pieces of string along the pattern lines. Where two pieces of string cross, cut a small gap in one and glue the other one in a continuous line, taking it through the gap (see illustration).

Coat the completed string decoration twice with a mixture of white latex paint, wood glue, and plaster of Paris. The filler in the mixture visually unites the raised string with the background. Now use a natural sponge to dab the reliefs with a variety of shades of green paint in an uneven pattern. Finally, use a thin sprinkling of sand, which is partially wiped off afterwards, to form a patina.

Rosette for the Door

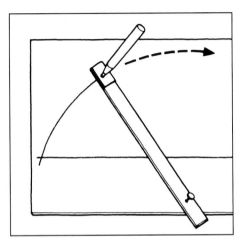 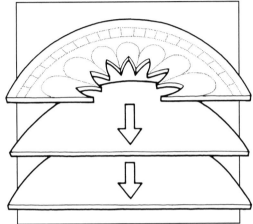 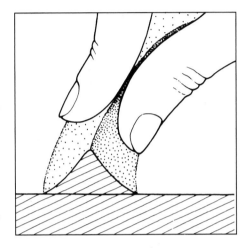

This rosette-shaped decorative element is designed as an upper section for a door or window frame. Paper "dummies" like these were used in the eighteenth century to create splendid decoration for the entire Ludwigslust Castle in Germany.

First draw the design for the rosette on paper. To draw the large semicircle, you'll have to make your own compass. Cut a strip of cardboard and punch a hole in one end to hold a pencil. Thumbtack the other end down and rotate the pencil in a semicircle. After making the sketch, cut out three of the basic shapes from heavy corrugated cardboard. Trace the pattern onto the uppermost piece of cardboard, using tracing paper. Cut out the surface of the inner rosette with a knife, so that three-dimensional depth is achieved. Then glue the three layers on top of one another.

Following the markings, apply paper mache pulp onto the raised pattern. Cover the background first with wood glue, so that it sticks better. Begin with the inside of the rosette form. Take lumps of pulp and press them firmly into shape between your thumb and index finger. Then add a rim onto the outer arch. It is best to let the work dry after each step; otherwise, it is very easy to spoil it. Then shape the outer border pattern with the help of a knife. Finally, paste paper strips over the outer edges of the piece to cover the cut edges of the layers of cardboard.

The rosette tends to warp when drying. You can correct this by pasting two or three layers of tissue paper onto the back. Be careful, because too many layers can cause warping in the other direction.

Coat the rest of the corrugated cardboard surfaces with a mixture of leftover pulp and glue to create a uniform look. Sand off any annoying uneven spots. Coat the rosette with several layers of white primer and, to finish, give it a patina with brownish matte paint.

Wall Ornaments Made From Plaster of Paris

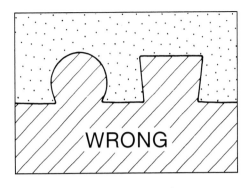

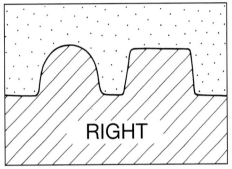

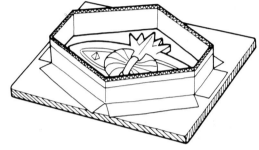

This three-dimensional ornament is made from a plaster of Paris mold. Any number of copies can be made from this mold. They can be placed on the wall or added to furniture—similar to stucco or wood carvings—to give an individual, stylish effect to plain areas.

You will need a basic clay form to make the corresponding plaster of Paris mold. This clay form is positive; the plaster of Paris is the negative form.

Sketch the ornament first on paper and cut it out. On a board covered with plastic, roll out the clay to about ¹/₂ inch (1¹/₂ cm) thick. Lay the paper pattern on top of the clay and cut out the clay in the desired shape. Then shape the additional details separately on the plastic wrap. You can remove them from this surface without damaging them and set them onto the clay surface. Make sure that there are no convex curves to get stuck inside the plaster of Paris mold later (see illustration).

The clay form does not need to dry. Construct a temporary frame around the clay form, using heavy strips of cardboard. It must be ³/₄ inch (2 cm) higher than the clay form and ³/₄ inch (2 cm) away from it on the sides. Protect the cardboard strips with wide waterproof tape on what will later be the inside, and then paste the strips onto the board around the outside of the clay form. Seal all joints with tape.

Carefully apply a coat of vegetable oil or petroleum jelly onto the clay form. Now you can pour the plaster of Paris. Start by spooning relatively thin plaster over the clay form, so that no annoying air bubbles stick to the clay. After that, pour the plaster of Paris over the entire form.

The plaster block must dry thoroughly before the clay form can be removed. Check to see if the plaster mold should be widened a bit at places where the clay gets stuck.

Seal the finished plaster mold with paint. Before using it, coat it thoroughly with hand cream or petroleum jelly. Then press small portions of pulp at a time into the mold, first in the deepest parts, then in the upper areas. Press the mass in firmly so there are no gaps.

The drying process can last a week. Keep checking on it. Thin sections dry and shrink faster than thick ones. This can cause the tips of the ornament to bend upwards somewhat. If they do, you will have to weight them down.

When the paper mache ornament is dry, it will shrink so much that it will be easy to remove from the plaster mold.

Smooth the ornament with sandpaper, if necessary, and paint it the same color as the wall.

Two Suns

These two suns, intended as wall decorations, have several things in common because they are both made from the same form. They differ, however, in material, method of construction, and decoration. Their faces show both friendly and threatening characteristics, because the line between the life-giving and the destructive power of the sun is a narrow one.

The source of both these suns is a three-dimensional clay form that was used to make a plaster of Paris mold. When the plaster mold was removed, the clay remained in one piece, so it was natural to layer it with strips of paper.

Shape the clay form on a flat board. An upside-down soup plate serves as the substructure for the curve of the face. After the facial features have been shaped, add eight broad and eight narrow, bent sunbeams around the face. Then construct a temporary cardboard frame on the board, coat the sun with vegetable oil, and pour plaster of Paris over it, as described on earlier pages.

The light yellow pulp sun is cast in the negative plaster of Paris mold. The finished mold must also be well coated on the inside with lubricant. Then apply about a ½-inch-thick (1 cm) layer of yellow-speckled pulp. The mouth and eyes are omitted. It is a good idea to attach a hook for hanging the piece onto the back of the forehead. Later, you can use it to lift the dried sun out of the mold.

Shape the painted sun on the clay form, which has stayed in one piece, using the layering technique. Before layering the paper, thoroughly coat the clay form once again with lubricant. Then you may proceed with the layering. The side edges of the sunbeams need special care, because they lend stability to the sun.

There are several steps in painting: put a coat of white on the dark primer and then a colored glaze. Sand the surface lightly so that some areas are bare and take on a worn appearance.

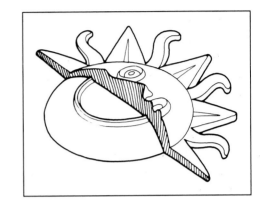

Flat Picture Frames

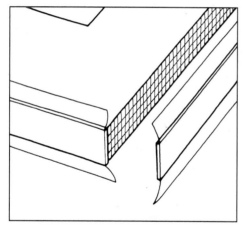

These frames are constructed from corrugated cardboard very simply, with no mitered joints. They are proportioned so that the frame is almost as wide as the opening for the picture. The simple flat frame has sufficient room for any type of decoration imaginable.

The frame is constructed from four layers of corrugated cardboard. Sketch the desired shape onto the cardboard and cut it out with a knife. Work the next three layers in the same way, but alternate the direction of the corrugated lines with each layer to increase the stability. On the two bottom pieces of cardboard, enlarge the opening for the picture $^3/_8$ to $^3/_4$ inch (1 to 2 cm). In that way, an opening is created similar to that in wooden frames, where a piece of glass, the picture, and a back board can be inserted. Secure the layers with waterproof tape (see illustration).

Paste all of the cardboard layers together with wood glue. Tape narrow strips of cardboard onto the outer and inner edges (see illustration). In this way, you create clean edges that will not bulge due to moisture when being covered with layers.

Now cover all sides of the frame with layers of paper, including the back side, to balance the resulting tension. Paste a layer of crumpled tissue paper onto the top to cover the uneven structure of the corrugated cardboard. Follow with two smooth layers.

Before pasting on the last layer, paste some string around the opening of the large frame as a border.

The large, patterned frame is decorated with many colors, using the resist method. The strips are covered with acrylic glaze, then simple patterns painted on with hot wax. Paint the entire surface once again with other colors (see page 187).

The little black frame is decorated with a sand pattern. Fix bands of sand on the background with wood glue, and then color the entire surface with black wood stain (see page 191).

Decorative Frame for a Mirror

You can decorate a frame with a dainty, ornamental outline and opening, then add three-dimensional ornamentation on the surface. You will find interesting inspiration for designs on windows and doors of historical buildings.

Sketch the overall shape of the entire frame onto paper and cut it out. This decorative frame is constructed on a substructure of corrugated cardboard, exactly like the flat frames on the previous pages. First, using the pattern, transfer the outline and the opening for the mirror onto heavy corrugated cardboard and cut it out. In order to give the frame the desired strength, cut three additional layers. The two bottom layers must be cut out an additional 3/8 to 3/4 inch (1 to 2 cm) to accommodate the mirror (see earlier pages). Alternate the layers so that the corrugated lines alternate between vertical and horizontal.

Always cut corrugated cardboard with a knife; shears will crush it. The cut edges of all the corrugated cardboard layers must together form a smooth edge, so glue a narrow, flexible strip of cardboard around it and then paste paper strips over it.

Now trace the decorative motifs, which will be made in three dimensions from pulp, onto the front side. To begin with, augment the outer edges of the frame with raised curves of pulp. To do that, roll out thick rolls of pulp, press them onto the background with a little glue, and press them into shape between two fingers. The strips of pulp will take on a triangular shape as a result. Allow this to dry first, so that it will not be disturbed by continuing work. Then set the spirals and wavy lines onto the surface in the same way. In place of a linear pattern directly applied, decorative motifs made separately from pulp could also be used and glued on after the object is dry.

Stress during the drying process can cause the frame to warp. This can be prevented by pasting two or three layers of tissue paper onto the back of the frame.

The rough form is now ready. Cover the various materials—corrugated paper, paper mache, and tissue paper—with a mixture of paint and leftover pulp to create an organic unity. This results in a slightly grainy texture. If you prefer a smooth surface, cover the entire surface with tissue paper layers.

The frame has a sand-colored primer. Using a toothbrush, very lightly sprinkle on the various colors which follow.

Sun Mirror

This sun mirror came about during a series of experiments I made using modeling techniques with the sun form. The two suns on page 124 and the mask on page 158 belong to this series.

For the sun frame, it is sufficient of course to shape just the circle of sunbeams from clay. As a base, use a flat board covered with plastic wrap. Roll out the clay on this surface with a rolling pin to about ½ inch (1½ cm) thick. Cut the sun rays out of this layer of clay with a knife. You can use a paper pattern to help. Round out and smooth the edges of the clay shapes with your fingers. Cut out the circular section using a pattern or with the aid of a plate.

Cover the clay model while it is wet. Cover it first with lubricant and as usual with paper strips. It is all right if the paper extends beyond the rays onto the plastic surface.

When the paper shell is dry, remove the plastic wrap. It is easy to remove the clay because it shrinks while drying. Cut off the excess paper around the edge.

The back of the mirror must be stabilized with corrugated cardboard because this form has to support the heavy mirror. Apply wood glue liberally onto the cut edges of the sunbeams and press the frame onto the corrugated cardboard. When the glue is hard, cut off the extra corrugated cardboard with a sharp knife. The opening for the mirror should be cut out ¾ inch (2 cm) wider than the opening of the

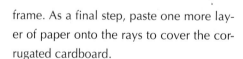

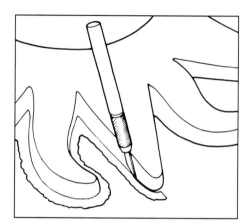

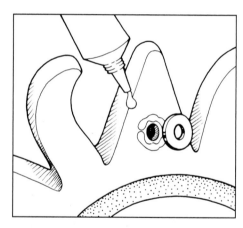

frame. As a final step, paste one more layer of paper onto the rays to cover the corrugated cardboard.

The sun frame has a greenish primer. Paste simple forms cut out of painted paper onto that. In addition, decorate the frame with sprinklings of color and dabs of gold.

Finally, set the mirror in. Have a glass cutter cut a round mirror with a diameter 1½ inches (4 cm) larger than the opening of the frame. Glue the mirror onto the

back side of the frame with silicon glue from a tube.

To make the hanger, punch a hole in the back of the corrugated cardboard. Because the mirror is heavy, you should use strong glue to glue a metal rim around the hole so that it cannot tear the cardboard. That way you can simply hang the mirror on a nail.

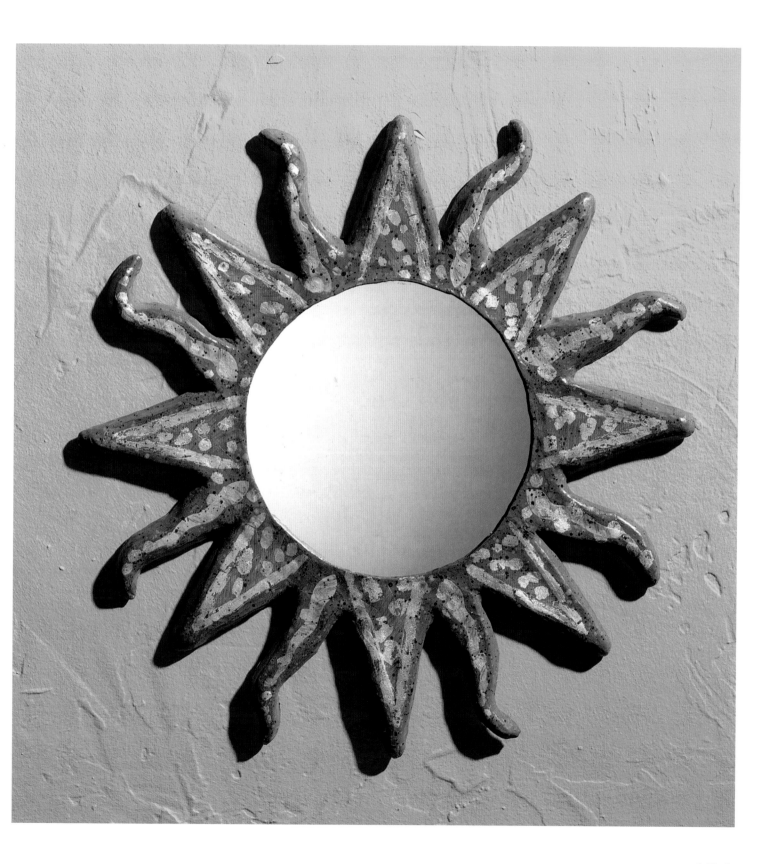

Swiveling Mirror on a Stand

Two well-mannered figures hold this little make-up mirror. The mirror is made of two parts—the moving mirror frame and the stand in the shape of a simple animal.

The mirror frame is hung on a horizontal bar. To be movable, it has to be balanced exactly. This applies not only to the upper and lower halves, but also to the front and back sides of the mirror. In contrast to the frames on earlier pages, this mirror is firmly integrated into the frame. It is symmetrically constructed. Two identical mirrors and two pieces of corrugated cardboard are needed.

Cut the cardboard so that the rim is ³⁄₈ inch (1 cm) wider than the mirror surface. Then cut the corrugated cardboard in half horizontally and stick the halves onto the back side of a mirror approximately ¹⁄₈ inch (3 mm) apart, using double-sided carpet tape (see illustration). The mirror must be protected from rust along this midline with waterproof tape. Repeat with the other mirror.

The area where the two pieces of cardboard come together later supports the bar. A metal bar about 6 to 8 gauge (3 to 4 mm) is suitable. As a substitute, you can use two pieces of thin floral wire tied together and

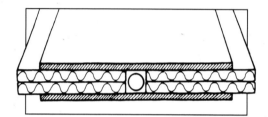

covered with tissue paper, as with the stand. With a large amount of wood glue, glue the bar firmly into the area where the two cardboard pieces come together because later it must not rotate. If the back sides of the mirrors are not protected, the glue can damage the mirrors! At the same, time join the two halves, back to back, with double-sided carpet tape.

Add a border of pulp on both sides of the basic structure. The paper mache must

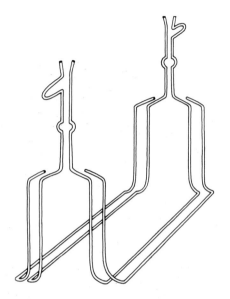

cover the edges of the mirror at least ¹⁄₄ inch (¹⁄₂ cm).

The stand is a wire structure covered with paper. It consists of four individual wire parts, whose shape can be seen in the illustration. In the area of the necks of the animals, bend the wires to form two opposing semicircles; together they form the opening. The individual parts are held together by winding thin wire around them (see also page 94). Paste crumpled paper strips around the stand. Pad the area around the neck and the legs a little more than usual and stuff the head with paper to form a rounded shape.

Paint the swiveling mirror with acrylic paint. A black speckled pattern is applied to a yellow background. Finally, apply varnish to the mirror.

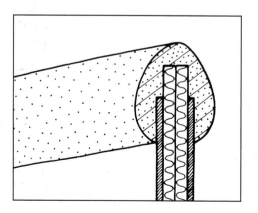

Lanterns on Wire Stands

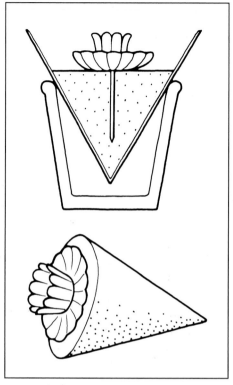

These simple, decorative lanterns consist of translucent paper cones supported by a variety of wire stands. The paper cones act as shades and as removable candle holders as well.

Construct the lamp shade from white kite paper. For each shade, tear into irregular strips one large sheet of kite paper and paste it onto the working cone (see page 62). Dip the scraps for the first layer in water and apply them. In that way you can carefully lift off the shade to check whether there are places that are too thin and must be strengthened. After drying, the kite paper forms a very firm, parchment-like skin with a somewhat irregular, crushed and very lively texture.

The candle holder sits in a plaster cone, which is set loosely into the paper cone but which cannot fall over. Cut a

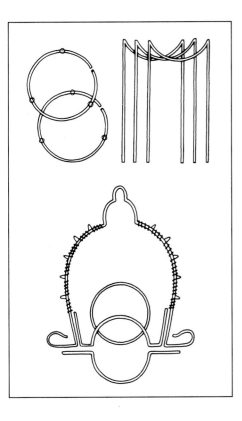

heavy piece of paper up to the middle and firmly wrap it around the working cone. Join the cut edges on the inside and outside with adhesive tape.

Place this temporary form vertically into a container and fill it with plaster of Paris about 2½ inches (6 cm) high.

Shortly before the plaster of Paris begins to set, press a small metal candle holder (the type frequently used in Advent or Christmas celebrations) or a piece of copper tubing vertically into the plaster. After the plaster is hard, the paper form can simply be torn away.

The shape of the stand lends the lanterns a simple, even playful character. All stands are made from bent wire and covered with paper. The shape of the wire elements can be found in the illustrations. See also Chapter 5, "Feet."

Four-Footed Lamps

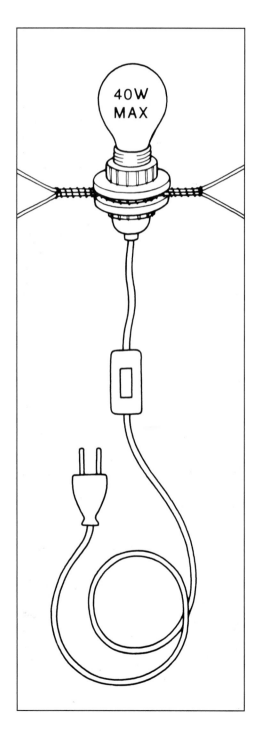

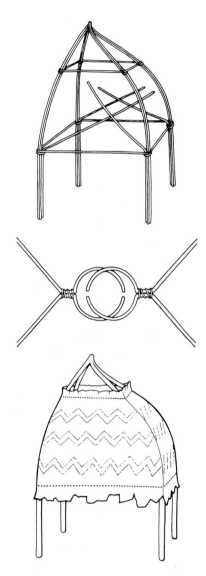

Now I would like to introduce several lamps, which are flexible enough to be placed on a table, window sill, night stand, or even on the floor. They are not suitable for lighting an entire area, but during the darker time of the year, they can create a cozy atmosphere. Do not be discouraged by the fear that working with electrical elements is too difficult. That is not the case with these lamps.

To be precise, the lamps shown are actually lamp shades whose corners have been extended to create feet. The four vertical legs merge into the tent-shaped shade and join together to form a diagonal peak. The four braces are made from double, 12 gauge (2 mm) wire. First join the wires temporarily with tape. For the legs, add a third wire which branches off at the height of the shade and about 12 inches (30 cm) of which is temporarily bent inward. Then join together the vertical wires to the cross supports above and below; this serves as the perimeters of the lamp shade.

After the stand has taken on its final form, wrap all the double wires with thin wire to join them together. Finally, bend the extending wire ends to form the holder for the light. Each of the two wires are joined together, attached, and then bent into a ring shape (see illustration). The ring must fit around the light holder. The two rings are joined together by wrapping. Cover the entire wire stand with paper strips in the manner described for wire feet.

Now finish the lamp shade. Cover the open surfaces of the stand. Since there is no surface on which to paste paper, you must create a temporary substitute. Cover the stand temporarily with plastic wrap (a cut-up plastic bag will do). Cut the plastic to fit, and stretch it tightly over the frame. Join the pieces together with adhesive tape and tape them to the framework.

Now you have a surface that can be covered with paper. It is best to use white kite paper, since the shade should be transparent. Paste two layers onto the entire shade. Allow the paper strips to extend ³/₄ to 1¹/₄ inches (2 to 3 cm) beyond the edge above and below. After the third layer, cut out and paste to the shade a simple jagged pattern made from white writing paper. Place a fourth layer of kite paper on top of that. Do not allow the paper to begin to dry out as you are working; if necessary, moisten it now and then. Finally, carefully remove the plastic wrap. Press the excess paper toward the inside around the wire and paste it down. It does not matter if the paper sags somewhat when it is wet; it will shrink up into a very tight skin when it dries.

For the electric parts you need a holder with two additional threaded rings for attaching the shade, a cord, a switch, and a plug. Take the parts to an electrician to avoid the risk of incorrect assembly. The socket for the light bulb is hung in the ring created in the frame and screwed in.

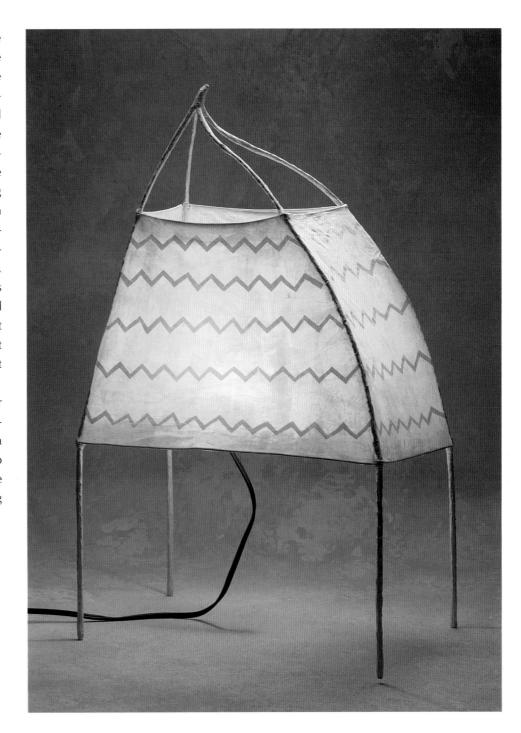

Green Lamp

This lamp consists of a base that is modelled on a plastic soft drink bottle, and a shade that has been built with layers of paper on a working cone.

Begin by preparing the plastic bottle for the base. First drill a hole in the bottom of the bottle for the cord and saw off the area for the threaded section with a small saw. Buy a brass holder with a switch from an electrician, two fixtures to hold the shade, a brass tube with screw threads (about 15¹/₂ inches [40 cm]), a three-polar cord, and a plug. Thread the cord through the bottom hole of the bottle, pull it up a bit, and thread it through the brass tube. Ask the electrician to assemble the parts that you have bought. The prepared bottle will then look like the illustration. Now fill the bottle at least half full of plaster of Paris. In that way the tube will be attached firmly in a vertical position in the bottle, and the base of the lamp will be stable due to the weight. Temporarily fill the hole in the bottle beforehand by stuffing paper into it.

Before continuing with the base, finish the lamp shade. The size and the angle of the lamp shade are determined by taking into consideration the half-finished base of the lamp. Construct it using a working cone appropriate for the base (see page 62), covering the cone with six to eight layers of white tissue paper. Follow with a layer of irregular paper scraps, which will lend a nice texture to the surface. Glue

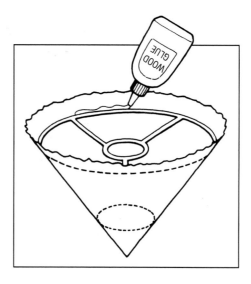

lamp shade rings about 13 inches (33 cm) in diameter to the top and the bottom. Available in craft shops, these rings provide stability for the lamp shade and a place to attach the lamp fixtures. Only then should you neatly cut off the shade about ¹/₈ inch (2 mm) from the rings.

In order to better judge the correct proportions of the lamp, place the shade on it. Cover the bottle first with white pulp. This changes the original form of the soft drink bottle somewhat. After the first layer of pulp has dried a bit, add little cone-shaped pieces as decoration.

Finally, paint the surface of the white paper mache with a slightly thinned oil paint in emerald green. Rub some of the same color onto the outside of the lamp shade as well. This causes the edges of the paper scraps to stand out in a fine network of lines.

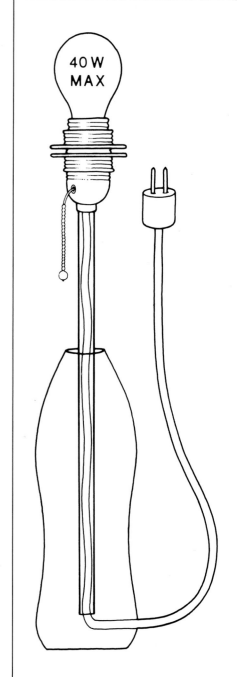

Lamps With Pointed Hats

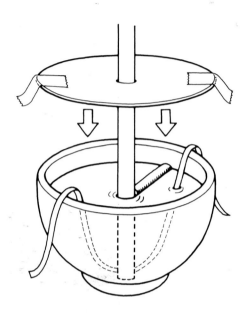

These lamps are interesting contrasts between clean form and playful decoration. The unifying elements are the tall, ice cream cone–shaped lamp shades. Reminiscent of the pointed hats women wore in the late Middle Ages, they can be decorated with medieval emblems and ornaments.

A round bowl is filled with plaster of Paris to form the base. Cover the inside of the bowl with a lubricant first. If you lay a band across the bottom of the bowl before you pour the plaster, you can use it later to pull the block of plaster out of the bowl. After the bowl is filled with plaster of Paris, be sure that the upper surface is level.

The lamp pole is integrated into the base. You must also cover it with lubricant so that it can be removed later. The pole is set vertically into the middle of the base while the plaster of Paris is still soft. It is held in place with the aid of a cardboard collar (see illustration). To create a tunnel for the cord, press a chopstick into the soft plaster of Paris.

The plaster block must dry out for one day and then can be pulled out of the bowl by the band. Pull the pole out carefully, cut off the ends of the band, and with a knife scrape off the uneven areas that may have resulted.

Now you can mount the base. Saw off the lamp pole diagonally to the desired length. Glue it into the plaster block with the diagonal end at the bottom and the threaded part at the top. Point the diagonal toward the tunnel. Thread the cord through the pole and the tunnel to the outside (see illustration). Then cover the base with a cardboard disc glued on underneath, and paste three layers of tissue paper around it. Put a narrow cardboard tube over the lamp pole and cover it with paper. If you cannot find a cardboard tube that fits, then you can make one from rolled up paper glued together. Now you can add the fixture, switch, and plug prepared by the electrician.

For the shade, you will need five sheets of heavy white tissue paper 20 by 20 inches (50 X 50 cm). Glue all the sheets together, so that you have one thickness of fairly heavy paper. This method of work creates folds in the layers of paper, but this is desirable. Cut the paper into the shape of a quarter of a circle—as if you were cutting yourself a fourth of a pie. To draw it accu-

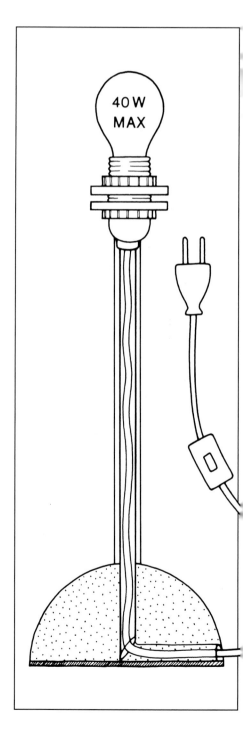

40 W MAX

rately, fashion a compass by cutting a strip of cardboard, punching a hole in one end for a pencil, and thumbtacking the strip down at the other end.

Now decorate the outer surface of the shade with randomly applied patterns made from silhouette motifs. Sketch the motifs lightly and make copies on a photocopy machine. Color the back sides of the copies with burnt sienna. Since the motifs are symmetrical, they can be folded together to cut out. Distribute them over the surface of the shade and glue them on (see also page 193). Apply a thin glaze of acrylic color in yellow and carmine red on the inside of the shade. The effect of the color will be visible when the lamp is on. Use the same color glaze for the base as for the silhouette motifs.

To help shape the cut-out quarter circle into a rounded cone, pull it carefully over the edge of a table. Roll it into a long, narrow cone by overlapping the two straight sides, and glue them together. Glue in a lamp ring at the bottom about 8 inches (22 cm) in diameter.

The shade has no opening at the top. This is possible because it is very tall; flatter shades require an opening at the top because of heat buildup. Use nothing higher than a 40 watt bulb.

Figures

Three-dimensional figures require support structures. These structures help hold the figure together, give it stability during construction, and define the shape. In this chapter I will introduce simple and more complicated support structures of cardboard, wire, and chicken wire and describe work with clay models and plaster of Paris molds.

- *Paper Mache Animals*

- *Birds With Crushed Paper Interiors*

- *Teddy Bears With Cardboard Frames*

- *Snake Bird With Wire Stand*

- *The Dragon*

- *Colorful Dog With Chicken Wire Frame*

- *The Watchman: Figure From a Clay Form*

- *Masks From a Clay Form*

- *A Second "I": Masks From Plaster of Paris Molds*

- *Fish From Plaster of Paris Molds*

Paper Mache Animals

Whether they're made of pulp or with the layering technique, figures require supporting structures. The figures in the following pages have simple or more complicated supports: cardboard or wire frameworks, clay or plaster of Paris forms, or even crushed paper. The supporting structures determine the shape and provide stability at the same time.

But first the exceptions. The menagerie shown here was modelled from pulp in a simple fashion. This is the easiest way to create figures of paper mache. The figures are rather small, though, and only two-dimensional. Paper mache pulp is not as ideal a modelling material as clay or plasticine, because it is not as finely textured. It has less toughness and weight-bearing capacity. Pulp is simply not suitable for larger, free-form objects.

Modelling figures does not require any detailed instructions. They are first shaped with your hands on a surface covered with plastic wrap and then smoothed out with a knife. The plastic wrap is easy to remove later. Before the animals are dry, you can coat them with glue; that increases the firmness of the surface.

If you want to make three-dimensional figures, it is possible to make them from two mirror images on cardboard patterns and then glue them together after they are dry. In that way you can be sure that the two halves will fit together. The little dog at the very top of the photo was modelled as a free-standing figure: even with a lot of patience, you will not be able to do much more than that with pulp.

Two-dimensional pulp figures can be made with the help of a plaster of Paris mold. This is worth doing if you would like to make several copies of a figure. The plaster of Paris mold can be made from a clay or plasticine figure. On page 162 there are instructions for making a plaster of Paris mold for a fish.

Birds With Crushed Paper Interiors

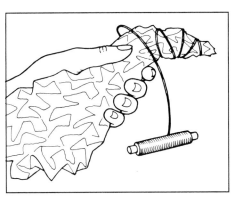

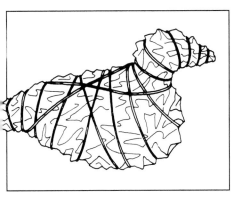

There is another simple way to create the shape of a figure, and that is to shape it out of crumpled newspaper. It is often hard to decide whether to consider this a shaped wad of paper or as material that can be used to make a free-form figure. In any case, the crushed interior determines the shape of the layered paper shell.

Crumple up two or three large sheets of newspaper to form a unified, oblong shape. By pressing it together, squeezing, pushing, pulling, and picking at it, make the approximate shape of a bird. Start with the head of the bird by pressing the end of the wad together. Hold the compressed section with one hand and, with the other hand, wind yarn around it to keep it in the desired shape. Continue with the neck and make a little curve in it. Then proceed with the trunk. This section is not compressed as much. Then it narrows down again to the tail. With one hand, keep pressing the wad of paper little by little into shape, while using the other hand to wrap the paper form. You can add a bit of extra wadded paper and wrap it with yarn in the area of the breast. The beak and the neck can be compressed even more by wrapping with additional yarn.

Now the bird shape can be covered with tissue paper. Use as little pressure as possible on the wad of paper; flatten only any unnecessary curves. The shape of the bird becomes visibly smoother this way. Interrupt the process after the fifth layer of paper to let the bird dry. When the surface has become firm, you can make small corrections and then finish the bird with five additional layers of paper.

The birds shown have a green primer and then are coated with a greenish umber color. White color is added on top. To create a vivid effect, do not cover the entire surface with paint. Then apply a light coat of ocher color and finally polish it with wax.

Teddy Bears With Cardboard Frames

A cardboard frame is well suited for these small and middle-sized teddy bears and can be created from simple materials. The cardboard structure forms a kind of skeleton. It is made from two cardboard parts that correspond to a front and a side profile of the teddy bear. The arms and legs are added on.

The shape of the cardboard pieces of the frame can be seen in the illustration. Cut them out of corrugated cardboard with a heavy craft knife. Cut the side profile vertically through the middle axis and join the two parts with strong tape on the front and back of the middle section. The arms and legs are attached in the same way (see illustration). Pad this skeleton generously with crushed newspaper. As with the birds, hold the paper form in place with one hand and with the other hand wrap it with yarn.

Now the teddy bear can be covered with paper layers. Begin with the larger surfaces and cover them with wide, overlapping strips. Wrap the arms and legs with narrower strips; use very small pieces for the paws. Take special care when covering the areas between the body and the limbs. After the first layer of paper, the body shape of the teddy bear begins to become evident. If necessary, you can add some more padding. Take crumpled tissue paper and press it onto the surface that you have covered with glue and pull it into shape. Paste paper strips over the padding without compressing it. After the third layer, let the teddy bear dry so that it becomes firm. Then cover it with an additional five to seven layers of paper. If the dried paper shell is still too flexible, add more layers of paper.

The two teddy bears shown are decorated with strips of newspaper pasted on crosswise. The paper strips must be covered with paste on both sides and soaked through so that they are flexible and can be pressed on firmly in the pasting process. Avoid putting any unpleasant print in the area of the face. The eyes and the snout are covered with torn paper with black printing. Small, white-colored flecks are added for the eyes. The newsprint can be colored with a watercolor glaze or a wood stain. Finally, coat it with varnish for protection.

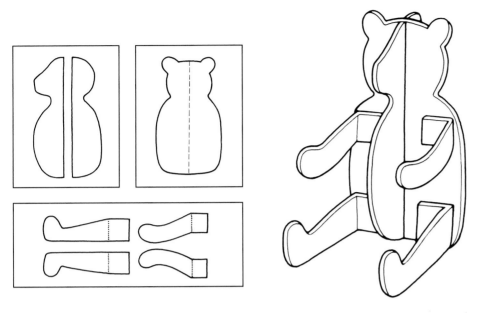

The Snake Bird

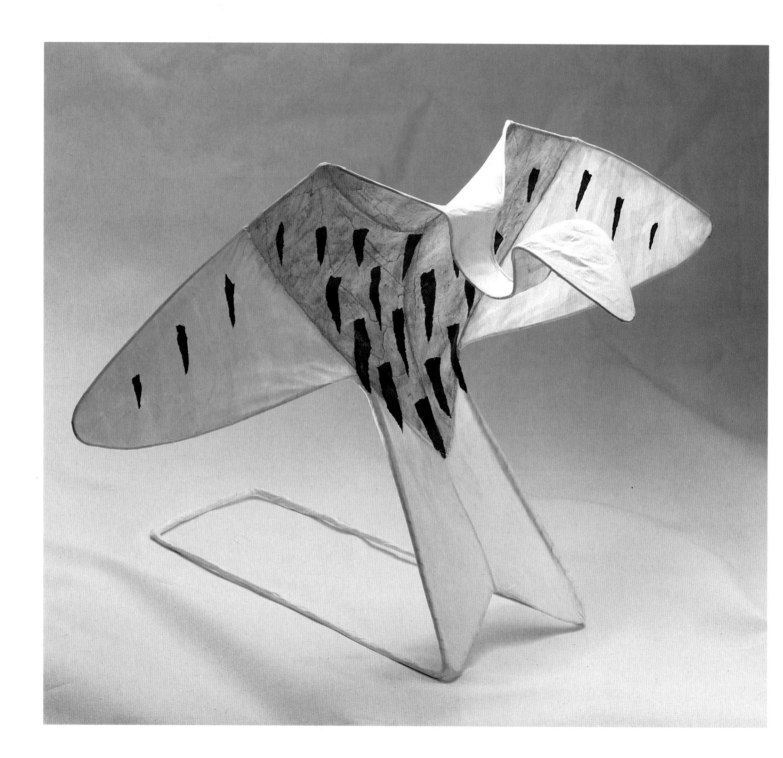

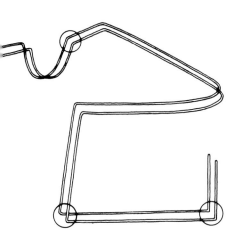

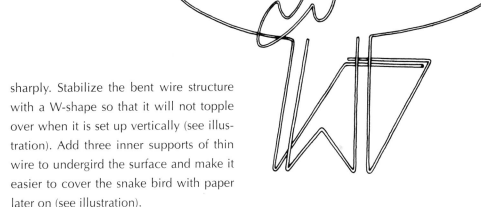

The next two figures get their shape from a support made by bending wire into various shapes. The wire forms an outline on which a surface is created by pasting paper on it. The bodies of the snake birds and dragon shown on the next pages have no volume. Although they are three-dimensional, they consist only of surfaces.

The wire support for the snake bird is made by bending a long piece of 12 gauge (2 mm) wire. First bend the wire together in the middle. The bend forms the tip of the snake's head. Then create the entire shape by bending parallel pieces of double wire as shown in the illustration. When bending the two halves of the wire apart, the three bends marked in the illustration must be bent in opposite directions. The framework ends at the bottom, creating a base that extends far backwards. Now bend the wire structure into its final shape. Make sure that it can stand upright and is balanced. Direct the body slightly backwards; the neck extends forward

sharply. Stabilize the bent wire structure with a W-shape so that it will not topple over when it is set up vertically (see illustration). Add three inner supports of thin wire to undergird the surface and make it easier to cover the snake bird with paper later on (see illustration).

Now tightly cover the body surfaces of the snake bird with white tissue paper. This is not the usual procedure for the layering method. Begin by stretching paper strips from one wire to another in the area of the wings and overlapping the strips from the two sides toward the middle, where the paper surfaces grow together. Then continue working in the direction of the neck and head and in the other direc-

tion toward the tail. While the paper surface is still wet, add another layer immediately. The entire surface needs to stay moist while working on it because if one area dries out before the others, some parts of the paper shell can warp.

The snake bird is decorated using simple materials. Color the white tissue paper in the area of the breast with red clay, and paste on scraps of black paper.

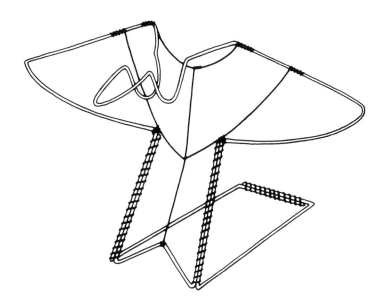

The Dragon

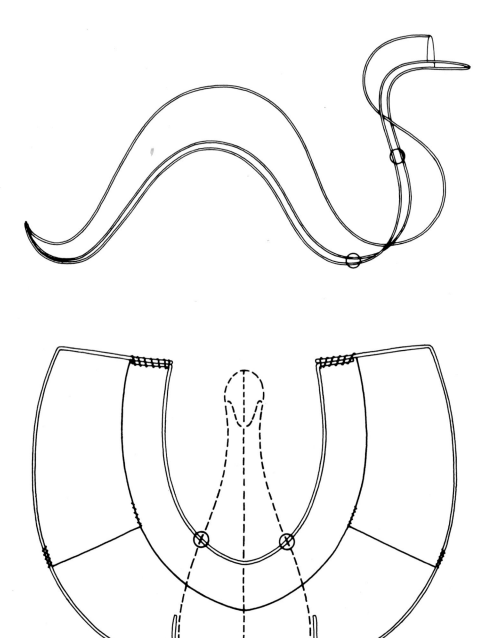

The shape of the dragon is also made from a wire framework. Even though, like the snake bird, it has no volume and consists only of surfaces, it creates more of an effect of a real body. This effect is achieved first of all by the up-and-down direction of the three lines that determine the two flanks and the spine.

Begin making the framework of the dragon with the three lines that determine the body shape. Join together three very long, strong wires at the tail end. Bend the two outer wires parallel to one another to form the wavy line of the dragon's body, and use the middle wire to shape the spine in a second wavy line that tapers off. The line rises up along the back above the flanks, curves forward in the area of the chest and back again at the neck, and ends at the top of the forehead (see illustration). The three wires are joined together by thin wires along the entire length of the body. This stabilizes the body shape.

Now make the head from thin wire. The ends of the two side wires form the lower jaw. Connect it to the forehead with a wire arch. Attach the upper jaw to the lower jaw also. Two wires leading from the curve of the forehead form the eyebrows and run over the back of the nose to the tip of the snout (see illustration).

Attach the wings at chest level at the lowest point of the bend of the body (see markings). The two wings are made of very long, strong wire. Fold them in two, creating two parallel wings. The connect-

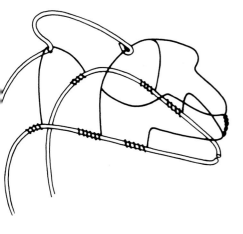

ing piece runs across the chest. Stabilize the wings also with two parallel, vertical support wires and one horizontal wire (see illustration).

Cover the dragon with white tissue paper. Stretch long strips of paper from one side, over the spine, to the opposite side. At the same time, paste paper strips up against these from the underside so that the wire framework is covered on both sides. Pull up the wings only as far as the horizonal support and leave the area underneath open. Cover the wire. The paper surfaces lend the dragon the appearance of having a full body because the body curves forward through the arch of the back and the breast bone.

Colorful Dog With Chicken Wire Frame

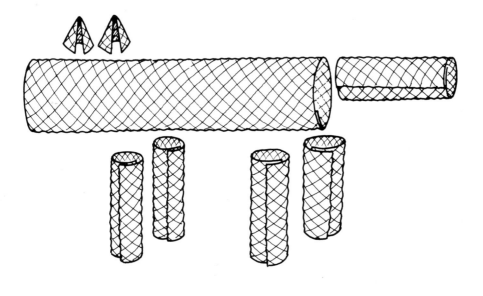

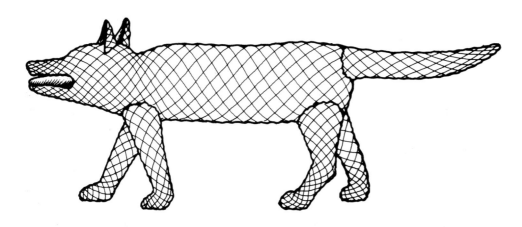

A supporting structure made from chicken wire is a good idea for large figures meant to have realistically rounded bodies, unlike the two previous flat, abstract figures. This type of structure is stable and better suited for larger surfaces than single wires or cardboard supports are. The exterior shape of a figure can be made to look very realistic with a framework of chicken wire. The dog figure is made from several parts constructed of chicken wire and then covered with layers of paper. It is advisable to wear gloves when working with chicken wire because it can easily scratch your hands.

First cut a piece from the roll of chicken wire which is somewhat longer than the body and the head together. Shape it lengthwise into a tube. The seam is closed using wire pieces and goes along the belly of the dog. Bend the back end of the tube together, press the neck section into shape, and press the wire together firmly to form a snout in the head section. Cut out the mouth and shape it.

Make the legs from tubes of chicken wire and attach them to the body with wire. Then bend the legs so that it looks as if the dog is running, and bend the ends of the legs forward to form paws. The tail and the ears are made as individual parts and attached. Needle-nose pliers are helpful

for the details. Finally, bend all wire ends inward.

After the support structure has the desired shape, you can begin to cover it with paper. Heavy tissue paper is best because it clings well to the form. Since the wire structure has no surfaces easy to attach paper to, begin with long strips of paper that can be wrapped around the entire body and legs and overlap at the end. Then join the resulting paper surfaces with large pieces of paper. Follow with an additional two or three layers of paper after the support structure is covered. The work goes quickly because you can use pieces of scrap paper.

When it dries, the shape of the wire frame becomes visible through the paper layer. To conceal the net-like texture of the wire, paste two layers of crumpled paper over the dog. Then paste an additional five layers on top of that.

Now stuff the dog's mouth—that is, fill the throat with wadded paper so that you cannot look down the dog's throat to his stomach. Paste paper strips on the inside of the mouth. Finally, form the tongue and teeth from crumpled paper.

Paint the colorful dog with yellow and red acrylic paint in several transparent layers. You can soften colors that are too loud with a patina: apply clear acrylic varnish tinted lightly with dark brown acrylic paint, then rub the surface (use rubber gloves). Finally, paste the teeth and the tongue in place.

The Watchman: A Figure Formed From Clay

In addition to using support structures of wire and paper mache, it is possible to use a clay model to make a figure. This is not exactly a supporting structure but rather a mold on which to form the figure. Like a chicken wire frame, a clay model does not determine the skeleton but rather the exterior shell of the figure. However, it is possible to define the desired shape much more exactly with clay. On the other hand, it is actually suitable only for small to middle-sized figures because it has considerable weight, which makes it hard to handle. Even though this figure is only 11 inches (38 cm) high, the clay model weighed almost 20 pounds (9 kg). As a rule, supporting structures made from wire or cardboard remain inside the figure. In contrast, the clay model is removed after the paper shell is dry. To do that, you must cut off the paper shell and put it back together again.

This figure shows a man who watches over a bowl. He is so engrossed in his job that he becomes one with the bowl.

First make the clay model. Place a large clump of clay on a suitable base that can be rotated so that you can turn the object as you work on it to reach all parts. In order to get an idea of the proportions of the figure, make a frontal and side sketch before beginning. Then cut away excess clay from the clump wherever there is too much and add it to areas where there is not enough. In this way you slowly achieve the desired form. The sketches prepared beforehand will help you do this. Last of all, scoop out the depression in the bowl with a spoon. If you interrupt your work, cover the clay figure with a wet towel so that it does not dry out.

Before pasting on strips of paper, coat the entire figure with petroleum jelly or hand cream. Then paste on about 10 layers of paper in the usual fashion. Because you cannot turn the clay figure upside down, the underside will remain open.

After it is dry, cut off the paper shell vertically along the middle line. It is easy to free these paper halves by pulling them apart from one another. If a figure is so detailed that the paper shell does not come off easily, then it is possible to cut right through the middle of the clay figure with a kitchen knife. Then you can remove the clay bit by bit from the inside with a knife.

Apply white glue all around the cut edges of the two halves and join them together. It is helpful to have a second person on hand to help because it is not easy to press the two sides together evenly all at once. Join the two halves with sturdy tape until the glue dries. Sand the seams a bit after the glue hardens and paste paper strips over them.

The watchman has a medium blue skin tone. This unusual coloring lends him a spiritual quality. He is then painted bright blue, the sash and inside of the bowl carmine red. Then paint over the entire surface with diluted gesso. The result is a surface more vivid and somewhat less bright than you would get if you had mixed the blue and white together from the start. Finally, cover the watchman's skin with black dots as decoration. Polish the figure with wax.

Finally, to round out his appearance, I gave the watchman a hat made from a simple little cardboard cone. His sash and hat indicate that he is a person of authority entrusted with an important job.

Masks From Clay Forms

Masks can serve their original function to be worn on special occasions, or, like sculptures, they can be freed from their practical use and serve purely artistic or decorative purposes. The two masks here are intended as wall decorations. Masks you can wear are on the following pages.

A clay model must be created for these masks. The shape of the mask has no real limitations. Museums of anthropology are good sources of inspiration. Masks of primitive peoples display varying degrees of alienation and abstraction.

Make the model on a flat board covered with plastic. The oval mask was made entirely of clay; the round one was shaped over a plate, which created the curve.

Cover the completed clay form with lubricant and then proceed by covering it with layers of tissue paper. The paper can be applied right onto the surface of the base. The many curves and corners require some care. Let the mask dry after 10 to 12 layers.

Since these masks are relatively flat and the clay model shrinks during the drying process, it is easy to remove the paper shell

in one piece. The paper that extends over the edges can be cut off. If you wish, you can stabilize the mask with a backing of corrugated cardboard. Trace the outline of the mask onto the cardboard so that the backing can be set into the inside of the mask.

In addition to giving a shape to the mask, you can express your artistic ideas by the way you paint it. You can give the mask a friendly, severe, lively, meditative, or wild expression in a realistic or abstract way.

The round mask looks at the viewer openly and full of expectation, perhaps even greedily; it is reminiscent of old Mexican artifacts. White paint tinted with a colored oil glaze is applied on top of a dark background (see page 186). A patina can be achieved by light sanding.

The oval mask has grim, almost warlike features. Instead of eyes, there are black and white stripes. Apply first a light, then a darker shade of color onto the surfaces, and then wipe off some of the color. You may apply a small red bead on the high forehead (see page 195).

A Second I:
Masks From Plaster of Paris Molds

One's own likeness and the possibility of changing one's identity have always interested mankind. Nowadays people portray themselves more readily through things, such as fast cars. But creating an identity from paper is much more instructive, more exciting, and cheaper.

If you wish to make a mask that can be worn, then you should make it using a plaster of Paris mold of your own face, so that the mask fits well. It is very easy to make this plaster mold with plaster wrap—strips of flexible fabric imbued with plaster, available at craft stores. Use a bathing cap to protect your hair. Apply cream to your face so that the plaster does not stick to your skin and apply ample cream to the front part of the bathing cap. Then cover your face in an overlapping pattern with plaster strips that have been dipped in water. Leave only your eyes and nostrils uncovered. To make a strong enough mold, continue with two more layers. Now you must be a bit patient for the plaster to set. If you move your face, the plaster will loosen and come off.

There are various ways to continue with the plaster mask. You can use the plaster mask as it is and cover it on the outside with paper strips; that way you will get a somewhat inexact model of your own features. However, if you paste paper layers on the inside or cover it with pulp, you will get quite an exact reproduction of your face. This type of self-portrait will

shrink as it dries, and you will not be able to wear it. In addition, the shape of the plaster mask can be altered with the help of clay. You can add clay to certain areas only or over the entire plaster mask. In this way you can change the mold, and your

facial features, more or less dramatically.

Before covering the plaster mask with paper or clay, protect it from moisture with paint. After applying clay to the mask, cover it with a wet cloth so that the clay will not dry out and tear. The upper surface of

that case, the two halves will have to be glued together again and the seam covered with paper strips.

A plaster of Paris mask of a human face is changed only slightly with clay. The features can be idealized or stylized by stressing the cheek bones, eyebrows, and eyes. Paint the mask with several uneven and transparent layers of umber and white. A fine network of lines, inspired by the tatoos of Maoris, covers the entire face of the mask shown. The coloration and pattern have a very meditative aura.

The same plaster mask was completely changed for the monkey face. Add enough clay on the chin and mouth areas so that they are pushed forward almost to the nose. Even out the area between the nose and the cheeks. Then shape the wide, open mouth and the flat sides of the nose. The eyebrows are intensified, protruding eyes set in, and little round ears added.

The monkey's face has a contrasting pattern that looks like face painting. It gives him a lively, friendly look.

the mask, whether of plaster of Paris or clay, must get a coat of lubricant or be covered with wet paper strips. Then apply about 10 layers of paper as usual.

After it is dry, you can determine whether the paper shell can be removed in one piece. If you are not successful, cut off only the chin section first. This was enough to remove the paper shell from the two masks shown.

Only with very complicated shapes is cutting off the entire mask unavoidable. In

Fish From a Plaster Mold

To close the chapter, there is one more figure that is cast from a negative plaster of Paris mold. In this case, it is a three-dimensional fish put together from two halves. The huge brutes are shown in the photo as they come out of the mold. Three-dimensional figures are always made by joining two parts this way. To do this, the figure is cut down the middle axis. The two halves do not necessarily need to be symmetrical, but they must have the same outline so that the halves fit together. Otherwise, the method is the same here as for the wall ornament on page 122—specifically, the clay mold must not have any bulges that will get stuck in the plaster of Paris form later.

First make a sketch of the fish in its original size and cut it out. Transfer its outline, one correct and one turned on the side, onto two waterproof boards with a permanent marker. Divide the clay into two equal parts before beginning your work so that the two halves will be the same size. The bodies of the fish must be fat enough so that the two halves together are rounded in a natural way. The tail and the fins must not be too thin. If you stick to the outline that you have drawn, you will be assured that the edges of the two halves fit together later.

Use strips of cardboard taped together to form a frame around the two clay molds. (The plaster of Paris, you recall, will be poured into this frame.) The frames do not necessarily have to be square; you can fit them to the shape of the fish with pieces of bent cardboard. Then coat the fish with vegetable oil and cover them with plaster of Paris. Start by spooning a very thin mixture of plaster over them, so that air bubbles do not form. Now you can pour the plaster of Paris around them completely. You will need at least 11 pounds (5 kg) of plaster for two halves of the fish, which are a good 16 inches (40 cm) long! The plaster molds need a very long time to dry completely. Then you can remove the cardboard frame from around the plaster

and remove the plaster block from the boards. Normally the clay fish will come free at the same time.

Seal the insides of the plaster molds with acrylic paint and then coat them thoroughly with hand cream. Then apply a layer of pulp about $\frac{1}{2}$ inch (1 cm) thick. You must press the pulp firmly into the inner surfaces of the mold so that you get a clean reproduction without any gaps.

Allow the fish to dry in a warm spot. Have patience. They will shrink while drying so that they will separate from the plaster mold automatically. Glue the big brutes together immediately after you have removed them from the mold, because the fins have a tendency to slowly bend toward the outside. If necessary you can sand the areas where the surfaces are joined with a large sheet of sandpaper.

Drill a small hole in the belly of the fish, which is now joined together, and insert a stick so you can turn the fish around completely for painting. Apply a white primer first, then colorful acrylic paint. The finished fish looks best if it floats on a metal bar with a base.

You can also make attractive wall decorations from the individual fish halves, which can be painted differently.

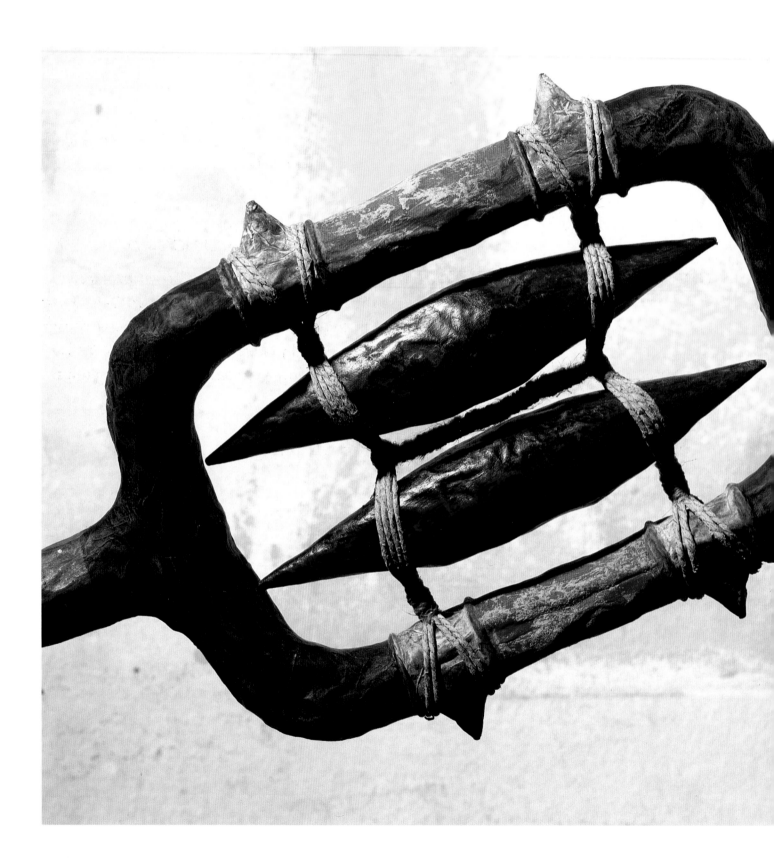

Free-Form Objects

In this chapter I will introduce purely decorative objects. They are a mixture of abstract art and tribal art. Of foremost interest is the formal, aesthetic aspect of the objects, because I am primarily a visually oriented person. But there is a certain charm in the relatively serious symbolic relationships.

- *Ceremonial Staff*

- *Animal Staff and Spiral Staff*

- *Four Spirit Houses*

- *A Shield Against the Evil Eye*

- *Oracle Spindle*

- *The Helmet of the Prophet*

- *Sand Cones and Spirals*

- *Wind Wheel*

Ceremonial Staffs

Originally, ceremonial staffs were not just insignias of power; they themselves embodied certain powers. Not only their aesthetic qualities but also the mysterious qualities attached to them have a strong attraction.

The three staffs shown here have heads similar to a lance, an antelope figure, and a sun spiral. As a group they are especially effective. All three ceremonial staffs have a core of bamboo and wire, which gives them their shape. First I will describe the lance-shaped staff on the left. The other two are on the following pages.

You will need a bamboo pole about 60 inches (1½ m) long. The head piece is set onto the staff. It is made of two pieces of heavy bent wire. Near the point they are twisted together, then they separate and form a kind of frame. Underneath they are joined together again into a vertical section, which is inserted into the staff and bound tightly to it.

The wire head and the bamboo pole are wrapped with compressed newspaper. In this case, the paper is not tied up with yarn, so that it has more volume. Attach the paper temporarily with tape. A second wrapping follows that. When the padding is thick enough, paste paper strips onto it in the usual manner. Work goes quickly using long, wide strips. After about eight layers, the covering will be firm.

The head piece has decorations above and below, around which a string will run later. They consist of paper mache cones that are pasted on and rings of cord, later covered with an additional layer of paper.

The head piece forms the frame for two separately constructed spindle-shaped constructions, which hang from the lacing. They are made from crumpled newspaper, which is held in shape with yarn and then pasted over with paper. The technique is the same as for the oracle spindle on page 174.

The ceremonial staff is painted in umber, black, and red. Rub clay powder into the red paint while it is still fresh to make the surface more vivid. Apply a glaze of thinned white gesso on the umber-colored surfaces of the staff and on the decorations on the head piece. In contrast, the separate spindle-shaped constructions have a shiny surface. Paint the exterior paper surface of brown packing paper first with a red to cover it, then with a black glaze. After that, sand down the uneven surfaces and polish with shellac. Finally wrap two shiny objects with string; they give the impression of being valuable jewels and lend power to the staff. Tie them firmly but so they hang freely inside the head piece.

Spiral Staff and Animal Staff

The two additional ceremonial staffs are likewise constructed from a bamboo pole and a head piece of wire.

The spiral, an old symbol for the sun, is made of double bent wire and then attached to the staff. The entire length of the spiral and staff is padded with crushed newspaper. Wrap the spiral a second time so that it is as strong as the staff. Then paste paper onto the entire surface.

The decoration of the spiral staff consists of two layers of color, one on top of the other, first orange-brown and then turquoise, which is partially rubbed off again (see page 188).

The animal staff has an antelope figure as its head piece. Its outline is made of bent medium-gauge wire. The figure stands on a horizontal base line, which is repeated in heavy wire horizontally below it. The curve of the antelope's body is filled in with wadded paper. Attach the padding with tape and paste paper over it. The detailed shapes require some care.

A bit below the crosswise support, integrate a paper sphere into the staff. It consists of a wad of pasted paper, which is pierced and skewered.

The decoration is made from thin, brown packing paper, which is partially

colored with black alcohol stain. The crosswise support below the animal figure has appendages hanging from it. They might represent something like votives brought to the figure. That colorful mix includes, among other things, paper cones, small pieces of branches, and narrow paper strips that hang on strings.

Four Spirit Houses

In many parts of the world, it is considered advantageous to offer your home to the spirits, to encourage them to spend time there, with the hope they will help the people who live there. These four spirit houses are associated with the four points of the compass, whose representatives they are meant to shelter.

The domes of the spirit houses are constructed with the help of a form made from chicken wire. Roll lengthwise a piece of chicken wire 40 inches (1 m) long, into a tube shape, and secure the seam with pieces of wire. Compress the wire netting in the upper area so that it gets narrower on top and forms a blunt tip. Wrap the tip tightly with wire.

Before pasting paper onto the chicken wire frame, wrap it loosely with two or three layers of newspaper that you have first wadded and then smoothed out (secure with adhesive tape). This loose padding prevents the paper layer from becoming too tight around the chicken wire. Turn the frame upside down on an upended bucket so that you can rotate it while working on it.

Because you don't want to paste the first layer onto the newspaper, wrap a layer of white tissue paper around the form first. Then paste over it with additional layers of white tissue paper. Because of the padding underneath, allow the paper shell to fit on the form a bit looser than usual.

The spirit houses have a pattern on the inside. After the first two layers of white paper, paste on black and red strips of tissue paper. The colored strips will be visible on the inside later. After that, continue to paste paper on the form until the paper shell is sufficiently thick (10 to 15 layers). The large surface area allows you to work with large pieces of paper, so the amount of work relative to the size is rather small. The lower edge is irregular and left rather thin at the edge. Finally, crumple the entire paper shell while it is still wet and loose, and let it dry like that.

After it is dry, it is possible to remove the spirit house from the chicken wire without bending it, because of the newspaper padding.

The wire frame can be used for the other three spirit houses; only the newspaper layers must be redone each time.

The spirit houses are decorated as follows: apply a white primer, then a coat of light green paint, and then a coat of terra cotta color. In addition, a design is scrawled on the surface with colored pens or pastels. Then sand the crinkled surfaces with a medium sandpaper until the green and white layers of the raised areas show through. As a last step, polish the surface with wax.

Finally, outfit the spirit houses with eight sticks that are as straight as possible. These lift the houses off the ground. Attach each stick at two places with hemp string; place a bamboo stick cut in half on the inside where the stick is attached to prevent the paper wall from tearing.

Decorate the insides of the four spirit houses with symbolic brush paintings, which indicate the four points of the compass.

A Shield Against the Evil Eye

As the name implies, this shield is not protection from physical attacks—it is too unstable for that—but it offers the bearer protection for his spiritual integrity.

The middle stick is the backbone of the shield, on which the entire creation hangs, and it also serves as a handle for the bearer. It was made from a strong branch of a hazel bush almost as tall as a man. The bark was removed only around the handle.

Attach the framework to the stick. To do that, wrap strong wire around the staff several times to make it firm; guide it to the left into a curved line toward the top, secure it there, and guide in a symmetrical line back down the other side. Wrap the wire once around the stick at the bottom and then guide it upward into an arch that extends forward. Secure it there (see illustration). This wire arch is tied to the cross supports with thin wire. The supports are bent slightly outward like ribs and positioned about 2 inches (5 cm) apart.

Behind the wire support, secure a thin branch horizontally with wire. The branches are behind the wire frame but in front of the stick.

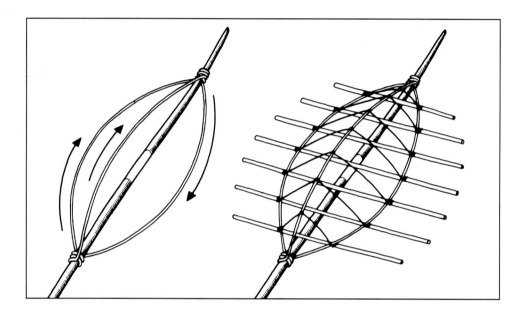

Now cover the entire wire framework with white kite paper. The shape of a ship will evolve. Stretch the paper strips from one wire support to the next, and paste them from the inside and outside at the same time so that the paper surfaces stick together and cover the wires. In this way you can cover the entire framework with overlapping layers.

When the surface is completed and while the paper is still wet, continue with two additional layers. You may have to moisten it again. The paper can sag a bit, as it will tighten again when it dries. The kite paper becomes very firm after only four layers but keeps its transparent lightness, which is essential for this object.

It is easier if you connect the outer ends of the cross sticks only as the final step. This fine wire line joins the branches that extend outward into an imaginary surface that encloses the paper-covered area.

The shield has no decoration. Its charm results exclusively from the materials used. Only the simplest, stylized decoration would suit this object.

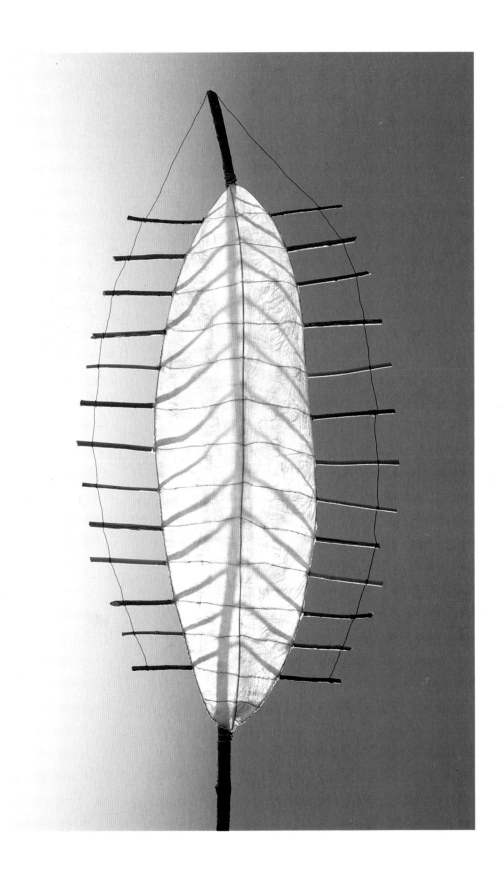

Oracle Spindles

The interpretation of oracles is common in almost all cultures. When they are spun, the spindles end up in a position that cannot be predicted, and a message can be interpreted from the random pattern.

It is easy and not very time-consuming to make spindles like these. You can make several at the same time. They are made from crumpled newspaper alone.

Crumple a large sheet of newspaper and then gather it up on the diagonal. This way the middle has more volume than the sides and the spindle shape results almost automatically. Wrap the paper mass together with yarn to hold it in shape.

Now wrap this elongated clump of paper with large scraps of tissue paper coated with paste. Try not to compress the inside shape. Wrap more firmly only the parts that bulge out too much. Wrap the narrow tips to form a cone shape. After about five layers, the surface becomes smooth and the spindle shape emerges. Allow the spindles to dry so that the sur-

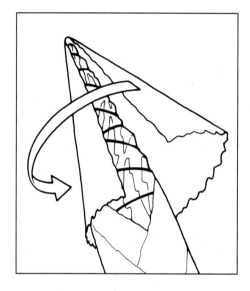 

face becomes firm. If necessary you may now make small corrections with crushed tissue paper. Then continue to paste on layers of paper until it is stable and cannot be compressed.

When the rough shapes of the spindles are finished, add a three-dimensional band of pattern around the middle. Gather into a coil paper strips coated with paste and twist to form cords.

Cut sections of this paper cord to make two ring-shaped strips to paste around the spindle. The surface that results can be covered with simple, abstract motifs. In order to even out the surface add two more layers of paper.

Coat the spindles with a white primer and then a transparent scarlet red acrylic glaze. Then coat them with a thin glaze of green umbra. The raised stripes of pattern can be emphasized with additional umbra.

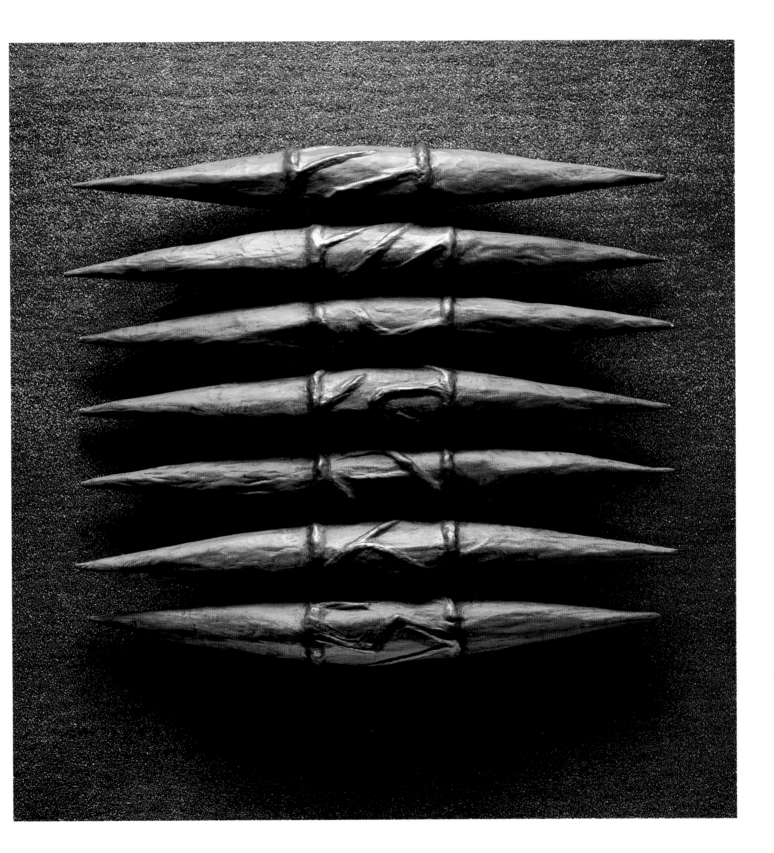

The Helmet of the Prophet

Helmets like these are used to block one's view of the outside world and to direct it inward, to allow the perception of visions. The helmet rests on the shoulders of the wearer and encloses his head. Breathing holes are added, but only away from the line of vision. The top is raised very high to make clear the state of the wearer.

The shape of the helmet is determined by a framework of chicken wire. Cut a vertical piece for the front and one for the back. The straight wires on the edges must be cut into at intervals so that the sides can be stretched out. Press the wire structure together closely in the area of the head so that the gaps between the wires become narrower. Then join the two halves together to form a tube, using small pieces of wire at frequent intervals.

Now form the shoulder areas by pressing out from the inside. You can press the wire network outward more easily if you use a hammer or a rounded wooden handle. Compress the wire once again firmly upward to form a point. Wrap the point firmly with wire. If the helmet is to be worn, you should try it on carefully from time to time.

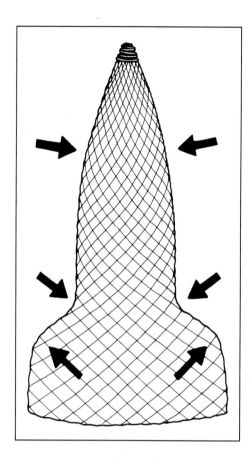

Place the frame onto an umbrella stand or lamp base to paste on the paper layers. This allows you to turn it and prevents the bottom edges of paper from getting crushed. Use long strips of paper running around horizontally, with the ends overlapping, so that the first paper layer sticks to the frame. You can complete the rest of the project, depending on the size of the helmet, by using large strips of paper. Use only eight layers so that it will remain light and flexible when worn.

After the helmet is dry, carefully bend the chicken wire frame toward the inside and pull it out. Unlike other shapes, forms such as these, which are open at the bottom, are easy to remove. In most other cases the chicken wire stays inside the object.

You may paint the helmet either before or after removing the wire frame. Divide the surface of the helmet into two areas with a black line. The inner area repeats the shape of the helmet, resulting in a figure within the figure. Paint the sides yellow, then cover both surfaces with black patterns. The surfaces of the inner figure have a lighter effect than the surrounding surface. This indicates the spiritual condition of the wearer.

To give the helmet a used appearance, rub it with thinned clay all over. The clay can be covered with wax so that it will not come off. If the helmet is to be worn, you must cut air holes in it. They are least noticeable if they are in an area painted black. The helmet of the prophet is most effective if displayed at eye level on a staff.

Sand Cones and Spirals

Sand cones look best if several are placed next to each other. Each is constructed from a bottle and a small, narrow cone. Use three wine bottles with narrow necks as described on page 52. Insert the small cone into the inside of the bottle form so that it extends out of the neck opening. The neck opening must be shortened a bit, since both forms are supposed to flow harmoniously into one another.

Then glue in the cone. Smooth out the transitional area with putty and then with a layer of paper strips. That finishes the basic form of the sand cone.

The decoration consists of a thin layer of sand. Coat the entire outer surface with a thick layer of glue. Then sprinkle the sand on the fresh glue so that it sticks. Add the black flecks with alcohol-soluble wood stain.

The spiral is a circular line in motion. It is one of the most balanced mathematical forms that occurs in nature and is considered a symbol for the sun in a number of cultures.

The spiral shown here has a core of chicken wire. You will need a strip about three times as long as it is wide. The strip must be cut in the direction of the roll so that the netting can be compressed. Roll the strips lengthwise to form a tube and press it together toward the ends. Now bend the chicken wire around an imaginary axis into a spiral. Press the wire together as firmly as possible at the tips.

The wire framework gets flattened when you work with it. To give the spiral some volume, pad it on the outside with crumpled newspaper. Secure the paper to the wire frame with yarn. Add a second layer of crushed paper in the center area. The shape of the spiral is flat on the inside and curved on the outside.

Paste layers of tissue paper onto the padded spiral form. Lay the paper strips coated with paste diagonally onto the outside of the spiral and press them lightly with your hands. Push the ends of the papers to the inside. When the outside is finished, continue with the inside. After a couple of layers, hang the spiral on a rod. The surface will become firm, and then you can flatten some of the irregularities or even them out with additional crumpled tissue paper. Finally, add more layers of paper un-

til the paper shell is sufficiently stable.

Prime the spiral several times with umber-colored primer, sanding it between coatings. Then follow with a coating of slightly thinned white gesso. Sand the entire surface of the spiral once again with fine sandpaper. This procedure transforms the rather lifeless white color into a vivid, organically graceful surface. Rub a thin layer of carmine red oil paint onto the inside. Allow the surfaces to dry, then paint on the black lines.

Wind Wheel

This wind wheel is much too unstable to actually function, but I like the fragility of this object. The spokes of the wheel are made of thin paper layers, which are attached to the rim by sticks and thin wire.

First construct the segmented spokes of the wheel. Begin by tearing heavy white tissue paper into 16 strips. It is easy to tear straight if you tear with the grain. The length of the strips corresponds to the desired radius of the wheel.

To make the wheel, you will fold all of the strips in half, lay all of the folded ends in the same direction, and glue the strips together like a notebook.

Brush paste on one half of a folded strip of paper. Only the outside should get any paste on it; protect the other half by placing a sheet of paper inside the fold (see illustration). Repeat with a second folded strip of paper.

Now press the two strips together on their pasted sides. The two folds must lie exactly on top of one another; the two strips of paper must be pasted to fit exactly on top of each other and must stick together without any creases.

Now coat one side of the glued pair and a third strip with paste, and paste them together. In this way the strips form a stack. Two single sheets will be left: one at the bottom and one at the top. These will be pasted together later.

Before drying, insert a clean sheet of paper between the layers of the stack to prevent the front sides from sticking to one another. After the stack is dry, separate the pages and join the two remaining single sheets so they can be pasted together and form a circle.

When you fan out the paper spokes, a wheel is formed. Decorate the wind wheel with black water colors before attaching the wire brace.

To fix the position of the paper, a kind of rim construction is needed. First attach wooden sticks to the ends of the papers. Coat a strip of each paper about ³/₄ inch (2 cm) wide with glue and wrap it around the stick. Then secure the stick with thin wire. Wind the wire around the stick twice, then continue onto the next stick and wrap that. In that way the distance between the spokes is determined. You can figure that out by multiplying the radius of the wheel by 3.14 and dividing by the number of spokes. You can also cut a small stick to use for measuring the distance between the spokes.

After you have completed the circle, tie the ends of the sticks together with wire all around the other side of the circle as well. Finally, thread the wire once again in and out around the wheel. The diagonal pattern holds the sticks vertical.

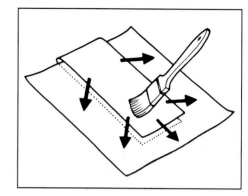

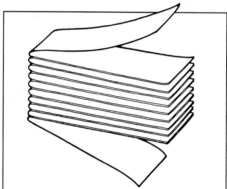

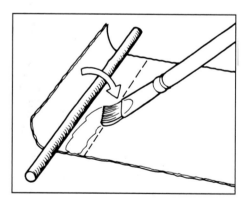

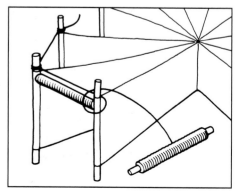

10

Surface Decoration

I am especially fond of the subject of decorating techniques because I like to experiment with a great variety of them. The effect created by an object depends on whether its surfaces have been fashioned in a convincing way. Creating decorations is partly experimental and partly a planned process; it almost always consists of several steps. All means available and all tricks of the trade are permissible.

- *Primers and Paints*

- *Painted Designs and the Resist Technique*

- *Polished Layers*

- *Sand and Clay Decoration*

- *Paper Motifs*

- *Appliqué*

- *Gilding*

- *Patinas*

■ *Primers*

Primers have the task of preparing porous, rough, and very absorbent surfaces for the application of paint. At the same time, they give the surface a uniform white color, which increases the luminosity of the coat of color applied later. They were originally intended for canvas and wood.

A primer is not absolutely necessary for paper mache. The paper itself, assuming it is clean and white, is a very useable base for all types of color. The primer covers and invalidates the character of the paper. For that reason, primers should be used only where they make sense: to smooth out a rough background or to cover unattractive types of paper.

Acrylic Primers: Actually intended for priming canvas, but also very good for paper mache.

Gesso: A high-quality, semi-chalk base, formerly made from bone glue and chalk, and used in artistic painting. You can purchase artificial, resin-based gesso ready for use at an artists' supply shop.

PVC Primer: This washable, abrasion-resistant paint is also available in plastic bottles in artists' supply shops, and a very good alternative to the artists' primers mentioned above.

All primers can be diluted with water but are waterproof when dry. They contain fillers, which even out the surface they cover. You can use water colors and acrylic paints as well as artists' oil paints on top

of them. To create a smooth surface, you should apply several coats of slightly diluted primer with a soft natural-hair paintbrush and polish with fine emery paper. Streaks result if the consistency is too thick or if you use a bristle brush.

Primers can be mixed with pigments and all water-soluble types of paints if necessary.

■ *Glazes*

Glazes—transparent paints—do not cover the object but rather allow the background to show through. But that does not diminish the intensity of color. On the contrary, glazes can create greater luminosity than opaque paints if the light penetrates through to a light background and is reflected off it. It is important to make sure you use a light background. This can be the white surface of the paper or a white primer. A pastel-colored primer is also a possibility—for example, pink with a carmine red glaze over it.

I like to use glazes to color paper mache surfaces without concealing their character.

Most types of paint can be used as glazes by diluting them. Both water- and oil-based paints can be used.

Acrylic Paints: Available as liquids in tubes or small bottles. So-called hobby paints in small jars are similar. All of them can be used as a primer or diluted and applied directly onto the paper as a glaze; they are waterproof when dry.

Wood Stains: Either water- or alcohol-soluble stains are suitable.

They should be worked with directly on the paper. If used as primers, they are absorbed and lose their color (see the bowl on page 32).

Artists' Oil Paints: I use only a very thin layer of these on paper mache. Use them either undiluted or diluted with a few drops of turpentine substitute and apply with a cloth or bristle paintbrush. An interesting pattern results on a paper background, because the torn edges absorb more paint and form darker borders. Oil paints require several days to dry thoroughly (page 53, right, Amphora).

Water Colors: These include gouache paints, water colors, and simple India inks, which are like glazes and can look very nice when applied lightly. They are more suitable for individual patterns or motifs than for a surface coating. They must be protected by a coat of varnish.

■ *Opaque Paints*

Fillers or opaque white is added to the pigments of opaque paints, which cover up the background. Therefore, opaque paint has more "body" than does a glaze. Opaque paints often seem slightly monotone. If I decide to use opaque paints, which conceal the vivid character of the paper, then I try to liven it up by creating a patina, by applying a glaze on top of the colored surface or by sanding it.

Acrylic Paints and Hobby Paints: These are very suitable for decorating paper mache when used as opaque paints, because they are waterproof when they dry. When a painted surface is thoroughly dry, you can paint over it without the original coat disappearing.

Gouache Paints: These do not have the advantages mentioned above and are not as advisable.

185

■ Decorating With Paint

In my work, I have never found it useful to decorate an object exclusively with coats of paint. In my opinion, using coats of opaque paint to cover an object always seems a bit artificial— which is not necessarily bad if it is done deliberately.

The example above is the Helmet of the Prophet (page 176). A flat, yellow coat of primer is under the paint itself. The bands are undiluted black acrylic paint. A patina is created by applying a thin coat of clay over the entire surface.

■ Painting With Glazes

The Mummy Case (page 112) is painted with liquid acrylic glaze directly onto the white paper background. The contours are drawn with a fine paintbrush with the help of a previous sketch. After the dark blue lines have dried thoroughly, the surfaces are filled in with magenta red and ocher yellow. The contours can be painted over without disappearing. The coat of colored glaze is somewhat uneven and results in a special luminosity on top of the light background.

■ White Highlighting

White highlighting is a painting technique used by the old masters. It was used frequently as a prime coat for oil paintings. But you can make it more striking. For white highlighting, a dark background is always needed. The motif is painted in white paint.

The Birds (page 146) were painted first with a green primer and then with a slightly transparent rough umber on top. The white lines were applied on top of that. The white is not completely opaque, so the decorative painting has a livelier effect.

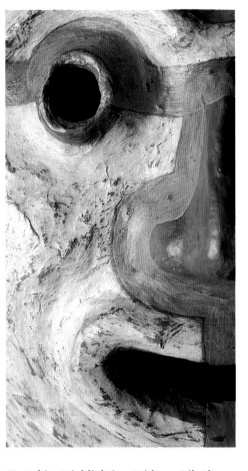

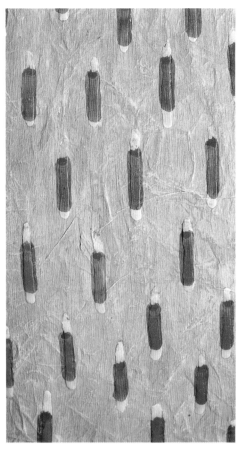

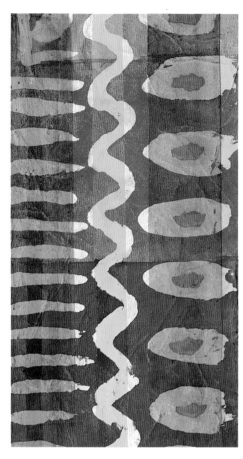

■ *White Highlighting With an Oil Glaze*

As mentioned above, white highlighting can be painted over with color. Acrylic or oil transparent glazes are suitable for this.

The Mask (page 158) is primed with a cold, dark grey with blended PVA paint. The face painting is done with broad, white, opaque lines; in contrast, the surfaces on the face are diluted white. A narrow, dark border between the surfaces is allowed to remain. The red painting is a carmine red oil transparent paint (glaze). A thin but undiluted coat of oil color is applied with a small bristle paintbrush.

■ *Resist Technique With Wax*

With the resist technique, certain areas of the background are covered with wax or latex so that they will not take on the paint when it is applied later. It is the same technique used for batik. Heat batik wax or candle wax in a can by placing the can in boiling water, and apply the wax with an old paintbrush.

The Green Basket (page 76) has a very simple resist pattern. The entire surface of the bowl is first covered with red lines. Then the red lines are painted over with wax in such a way that the wax lines extend be-

yond the red. After that, the entire bowl is painted green. The red lines, and their white ends, do not take on the green color.

Green and yellow lines were first drawn around the Picture Frame (page 127). A simple pattern was painted on, using liquid wax. The frame was painted over again, section by section, with violet, magenta, and orange. Acrylic glazes produce charming mixed colors when applied one on top of the other.

The wax can be removed by ironing it or by scraping it off. Polishing with paste wax gives the entire surface an even sheen.

187

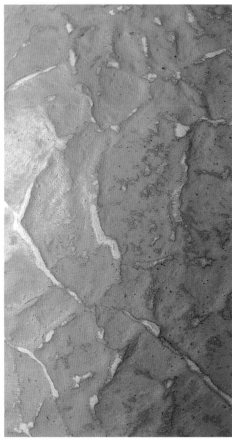

■ *Layers of Sanded Paint*

If you apply several different layers of paint to an uneven background and then sand the surface with sandpaper, the underlying layers of color on the raised area of the surface will be exposed again. The effect can be very different, depending on the texture of the background. The photo shows the surface of one of the Spirit Houses (page 170), where even part of the top layer of paper is sanded off.

■ *Layers of Sanded Gesso*

Here as well, successive layers are sanded down. In this case, gesso is used. The layers are thicker because of the high content of filler. Three coats of white gesso are applied on the slightly uneven surfaces, followed by two coats in reddish tones, and finally two in turquoise-green. Little islands, white inside and reddish outside, become visible on the turquoise surface (Bowl, page 38). For adding color to gesso, you can use pigments or even acrylic paints.

■ *Layers of Rubbed Paint*

A further variant is a technique that can be described as a process of energetic wiping or light rubbing with a cloth. A primer of acrylic paint is applied and allowed to dry thoroughly. Then a coat of another color is applied over that, a line pattern as shown here (the stand on page 89). When the upper layer of paint has dried slightly, wipe off the raised parts with a wet cloth. You must test the amount of pressure to apply so that you do not wipe off too much or too little paint.

Wiped Oil Pastels

Technically, this is also a resist technique, but it results from wiping away color. Holding a pastel crayon flat, rub it over an uneven surface so that the pastel sticks to the raised parts. Then paint over the pastel with diluted acrylic paint. Later, rub the surface with a cloth, thus removing the acrylic paint from the specks of pastel (see the case on page 110). The best result is achieved if you work on a light background and choose a pastel in a light color that is related to the acrylic's hue. Contrasting pastels leave ugly traces.

Sanded Color Inlay

Prime the background twice with gesso and sand it. Cut a stencil from heavy cardboard for the design. Mix red clay or pigment into undiluted gesso. Put the stencil in place and hold it down firmly with two fingers. Then use a knife to apply the color mix inside the borders of the stencil. Lift the stencil off, being careful not to smear the fresh paint. Now the motif is created by a raised layer of color. If necessary, clean the back of the pattern before using it again. Mistakes can be scraped off with a sharp knife.

Coat the entire object with three layers of gesso with blue color added, and, after it is thoroughly dry, polish it with emery paper until the raised motifs come to light again (see the pedestal on page 92).

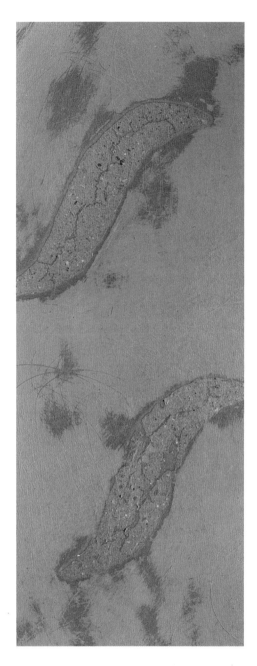

■ Clay on a Grainy Background

You can collect clay in many shades of color from your own area or on trips. It is pulverized or dissolved in water and rubbed onto a matte surface. The effect varies according to the nature of the background.

This example (the bowl on page 40) has an effect similar to sandstone. An uneven paper surface is coated with a mixture of coarse putty and wood glue. The reddish clay is wiped on sparingly with a cloth.

■ Earth Colors

You can create earth tones yourself from pulverized, colored clay by adding a binder. A synthetic resin binder is suitable, like that used for powdered paints, or adhesives like wood glue or paste, as well. The earth colors can used on a flat surface or for motifs and patterns. The colors are not entirely opaque, so the color applied on top has a very lively effect (for example, see the Snake Bird on page 150).

■ Sand Applications

Sand can be fixed to a background with the help of a binder. In contrast to clay, sand does not dissolve in water and for that reason has no coloring property, but rather creates a grainy texture. The example shows completely normal sifted garden soil on white paper.

You can use sand to give a rough texture to surfaces so that they can be painted. You can also mix it with paint or put it on top of an existing layer of paint to form a patina (for example, the wall relief on page 116).

■ Sandpaper

Here the background is covered with a thick layer of sand. Sand exists in a great variety of colors, too. Any kind of sand is suitable, from very fine to grains of about $1/16$ inch (1.5 mm) (possibly washed and sifted). Apply a thick coat of wood glue to the entire surface of the object and sprinkle a generous amount of sand onto the fresh glue. After it dries, you can tap the object lightly to remove the excess sand. The surface will remain somewhat crumbly, so it is not wise to touch it too often (see the sand cone, page 178).

■ Sand Pattern

Sand can also be glued to certain specific areas. Paint the pattern or motif onto the object with wood glue, using a paintbrush (possibly make a pencil drawing beforehand). When the sand is sprinkled on, it sticks only to the surfaces coated with glue. It is better to work on one area at a time when applying sand patterns to larger surfaces, so that the glue does not dry too quickly.

Afterwards, the sand can be painted. Alcohol-based stain is very suitable for that. On different surfaces, the black stain used here creates various qualities of color, which change over into violet tones in an attractive way (see the frame, page 127).

■ Fake Sand

You can also create fake sand. First apply a coat of beige primer. Then apply dabs of heavily diluted raw umber with a natural sponge. Add fine speckles of paint on top of that with a toothbrush.

For the example shown (the frame on page 128), various mixtures of umber and burnt sienna were used first, then a little yellow and orange, then a little black, and finally white.

191

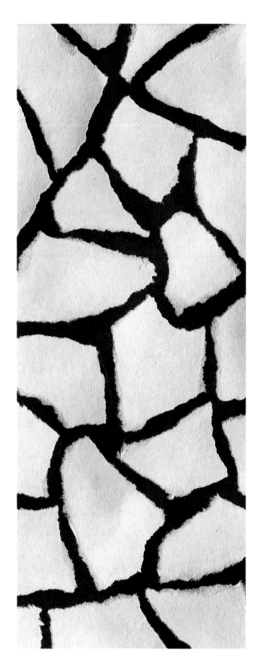

■ Mosaics

In addition to painting, pasting on cut or torn paper motifs is also interesting. You can use individual motifs in a random pattern.

One of the many possible patterns is the mosaic, which is made from either torn strips, as in the photo (the Octopus, page 98), or from little pieces of cut paper. If you use cut paper pieces, you get the effect of a mosaic made of broken glass or pottery shards. You can use a mosaic as a random pattern to cover a surface or create borders and motifs similar to those on old floors.

■ Painted Paper

The design possibilities are often freer and more variable if the motifs are not painted directly onto the object but rather painted onto paper and then pasted on. The design can be tested out by playing with it and moving it back and forth on the object.

There are two possibilities: You can cover the entire paper with painted patterns and cut figures from it. Or you can paint the motifs on the paper and cut them out, leaving the desired amount of border around the pattern. In that way, the colored surface of the border area is included in the design.

The example at right (the bowl on page 44) shows white motifs that have been painted on paper primed with black. They were torn out and pasted onto an orange-colored background. For this approach it is best to use heavy, white tissue paper and to prime it in the desired color. With colored tissue paper, the colors will fade.

Water-soluble paints should not be used for painting the designs; they will be ruined when the paper is pasted on.

■ Cut-Out Motifs

In contrast to torn motifs, cut silhouettes have a clean look because of their strong outlines. Either random patterns or single figured motifs can be used; think of the silhouettes by Matisse.

The example at left (the lamp shade on page 141) shows a section of the lamp shade; its surface is covered uniformly with symmetrical ornaments. They were sketched lightly beforehand and copied on a photocopy machine; then the back sides of the copies were colored with acrylic paint. The ornaments were folded together and cut out along the middle lines—which saved half the work and assured uniformity.

To paste on delicate paper shapes, apply paste to the background surface only, not to the silhouette. If pasted directly, the silhouette will become limp and unwieldy, and you won't be able to position it accurately.

■ The Sandwich Technique

In this variation, the cut-out motifs are enclosed between the background and a paper layer pasted on top of it. They either show through or have a raised surface that shows the shape.

The example (the bowl on page 48) has a random pattern of animal figures and circles. They are white, structured, handmade paper pasted onto a blue background and pasted over with very thin, transparent tissue paper. Finally, the top surface is rubbed with diluted blue oil paint.

A simple surface can gain a three-dimensional character by the application of additional materials. Sewing and pasting are the main types of appliqué techniques.

■ *String Decoration*

The pattern on the red basket (page 77) has been sewn on with thin sisal string. The finished string pattern is coated with a mixture of grainy putty, wood glue, and PVA primer. This mixture sticks mainly to the raised strings and joins them together visually with the background. A coat of thin, orange-colored acrylic paint is applied over the primer. Finally a thin coat of carmine red oil paint is rubbed on with a bristle paintbrush.

A second possibility is to create lines or patterns with ordinary package string. The pieces of string are cut to fit and glued onto lines that have been sketched onto the object. Then they are coated with a primer that has plaster of Paris in it (see the wall relief on page 116).

■ *Sewn Cord*

Whereas the primer unifies the background with the string to form a relief in the examples above, here the texture and the sheen of the cord, which is sewn on, creates the central focus (see the bowl on page 38). Sketch the crooked line on lightly. Poke holes along the line about 1/2 inch (1 cm) apart. Then sew on the white cord with green embroidery floss. The yarn is threaded from the inside from one hole to the next; on the outside it loops around the cord and is then threaded back through the same hole again to the inside. The ends of the cord are pulled through an opening and glued on firmly.

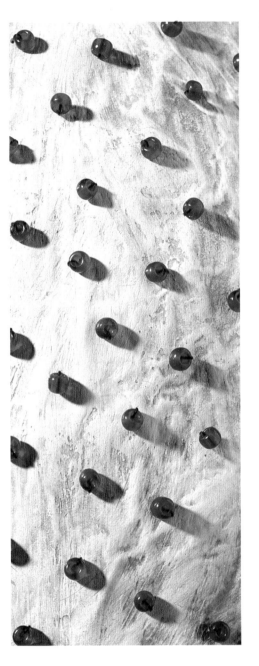

■ *Appliquéd Beads*

The mask on page 158 has red glass seed beads sewn on in the area of the forehead. First distribute the holes equally on the surface by pricking with a needle. Then sew the beads on with thread, going from one bead to the next while keeping the thread on the back side.

In addition to various types of beads, short, hollow twigs or pieces of bamboo sticks can be sewn on. Also, small feathers, seedpods, squash seeds, pieces of bark, brass disks, little pieces of leather, or pine cones can give an interesting appearance if they are appliquéd to a suitable object.

■ *Knots and Fringes*

The pod case (page 114) is decorated with sisal string that does not lie flat but stands out in a bushy fashion. To achieve this, knot a piece of sisal string in the middle and bend it in half. Thread both ends of the string from the outside through a hole that has been drilled beforehand, then knot it once again. Then twist the ends of the strings apart, so that the inside of the pod is covered with a profusion of fringes. The red knots form a subtle, looped pattern on the polished outside of the object.

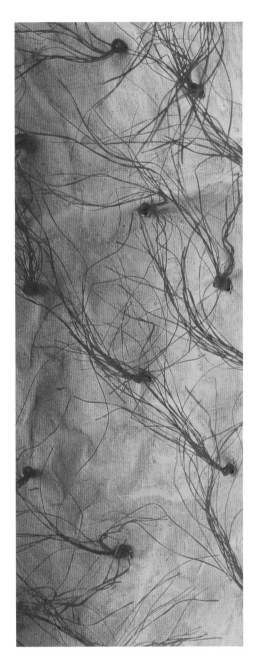

Gilding

There are two different methods for gilding with gold leaf: the highly lustrous water gilding, and the duller (more matte) oil gilding. The more lavish type is water gilding, but it takes long years of experience to learn. I will describe the easier method of oil gilding here.

Gold leaf is real gold hammered into extremely thin leaves—.0001 millimeter thick! It is so fine that it is transparent and tears when handled. Gold leaf comes in booklets, with the leaves sandwiched between pieces of paper.

Also available is artificial gold leaf made from a gold-colored metal alloy, which is known as beaten metal or composition leaf. Not only is composition gold much more reasonably priced, it is not as thin, so it is easier for the nonprofessional to use. In addition to gold leaf, there are also authentic silver leaf and the substitute, aluminum leaf.

Beaten metal and silver leaf tarnish with time. To prevent that, you can coat the object with cellulose lacquer. Gold color gets darker over time if not sealed.

For gilding, a special oil-based adhesive, called *size*, is used to fix the gold to the object. It is available with different drying times—for example, three, six or 12 hours. At the designated time, the size becomes *tacky*—that is, almost dry— which is the right consistency for applying the gold.

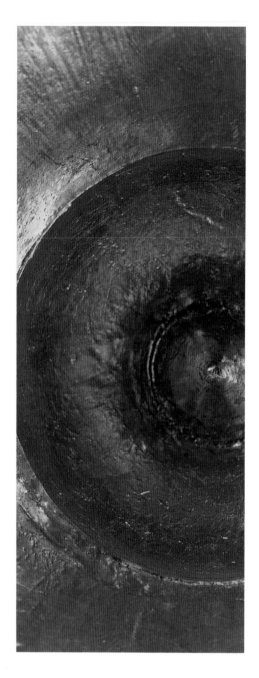

To achieve the best possible effect, a completely flat background is needed. Every grain and uneven area will show through later. Before the size is applied, the background must be primed and sanded several times. Then it is coated with ocher or red paint. If the base is very absorbent, you can also add a thin coat of clear varnish so that the size is not absorbed into the surface.

Apply the size evenly. The gold will not stick to places where it is not deliberately applied. Do not allow the surface to get dusty during drying.

When the size is almost dry, the right time has come to apply the gold leaf. To test whether it is ready, run your finger over the surface; if it "whistles"—that is, if you hear a kind of squeaking sound—the size is the right consistency. If the drying process has progressed too far, the gold will no longer stick.

To apply the gold, slide it out of the booklet onto a piece of paper. (If necessary, it can be cut together with the paper pages of the booklet.) Then push it out a little over the edge of the paper with a wide, flat paintbrush. Then push the gold leaf into the desired position, allowing the excess to extend out beyond the edges. Pull the paper out from underneath the gold leaf. All of this must be done very slowly—it's wise to hold your breath—or the gold will fly off.

Now dab (don't stroke) the gold leaf firmly into place with a ball of cotton. After a few additional hours, when the size is

thoroughly dry, remove the excess gold by wiping the surface softly with a ball of cotton and polishing the gold.

Since paper mache tends to have irregular and uneven surfaces, do not expect a perfect result. (See the goblet on page 54.)

You will see examples of gilding today that have gaps or look torn to produce an antique or used look. This is actually the result of improper and hurried gilding, but it also has its charm. The gold is laid in the size while it is still soft, so that it can still be moved around a bit. This is how the tears and gaps result on the uneven background. To enhance the effect of this type of gilding, the gold is applied onto a contrasting color, for example carmine red, turquoise, or dark blue (see the bowl on page 35).

Gilding can also be used on certain selected areas as decorative strips or as a pattern. In this case, all surfaces where the gold should stick must be coated with the size. It is helpful to color the size with a little yellow oil paint so that it is more defined. Be very careful when cutting the gold leaf into narrow strips. Rub your brush lightly over your cheek to pick up a bit of oil, then pick up the gold with the brush and place it in the desired location. Rub off the excess gold when it is dry (see the goblet on page 55).

■ *Patina*

The purpose of patina is to give an object an old, used appearance, thus lending it a certain flair. It gives life to an uninteresting surface and enhances the three-dimensional surfaces like reliefs. The best-known is the dark patina, which can be purchased ready to use in bottles. As a substitute, you can use a clear varnish with a small amount of color added, or you can rub the surface with watery, diluted acrylic paint. You can also mix fine sand with wood glue and apply it. While the patina is still fresh, wipe it off the raised areas with a cloth.

The example above left (the rosette on page 120) shows a relief painted white, then covered with a brownish-tone clear matte varnish.

Light patina, which gives an object a dusty, faded appearance, is not as well known. The entire object is given a coat of very diluted gesso milk. The matte, chalky white of the gesso has a powdery effect. A glossy sealant would not be advisable for this.

The light blue bowl (page 51) combines several techniques. It has a brownish primer, followed by a light blue coat, then the dark brown motifs, and finally a coat of white gesso. Finally, the bowl was sanded lightly.

A further possibility is to distribute speckles over a surface, giving it a rough, porous appearance. Use a toothbrush or a nail brush for this. Spread some paint on the brush and run your finger over the brush. If there is too much paint on it, you will get blobs instead of speckles.

The strong orange and green tones in the example (the bowl on page 35) are softened with a thin coat of sandy color, which has been wiped off and speckled with umber.

Sealing

Another way of making an object appear used is to sand it. To achieve the desired effect, a darker color must be underneath the layer of color to be sanded off; the sanding brings it to light. This type of treatment must be planned in advance as well. The monkey mask (page 160) was pasted over with packing paper before it was painted, then sanded after that.

Sealants are used both to protect the surface and to make the colors more intense. Clear varnish provides the hardest protective coating. In addition, there are several lesser-known alternatives, which give the surface a softer, more natural sheen.

■ *Varnishes*

These are the most common means of protecting painted surfaces. There is a synthetic resin varnish, which can be diluted with turpentine substitute, and an acrylic varnish, which can be diluted with water. Both are available in high gloss or matte finishes. The varnish must not dissolve the paint underneath it. Water-soluble colors should be varnished with synthetic resin varnish. Both types are suitable for acrylic paints, and oil paints can be varnished with both types as well, provided they have dried for an entire month.

I prefer the matte varnishes, because highly glossy varnishes develop a very artificial, polished film, which in my opinion does not suit paper mache very well.

■ *Paste Wax*

This gives an especially fine, silky sheen. In contrast to synthetic resin varnish, it does not make the color darker. One or two thin layers of wax are applied with a cloth or a brush. After a short time, you can polish with a cloth using only light pressure. Sealants that shine only when polished take on a high sheen on the raised places and remain dull on the low-lying parts, just like old objects that have been worn to a sheen.

■ *Shellac*

What is true of wax is true of shellac. The uneven surfaces characteristic of paper mache are emphasized by various degrees of sheen. You can apply it with pieces of cloth folded up into balls. (Check the manufacturer's instructions on the label.) The saturated balls are moved over the surface with quick circular movements, and this creates the sheen. The balls cannot touch the surface for long or they will stick. Depending on how high a sheen you wish, you must apply two or more layers. If the balls are to be used again, you can keep them several weeks in a glass jar. Shellac is advisable mainly for a dark background because it has a light brown color itself.

Materials & Tools for Surface Decoration

Adhesives: Paste is used to attach paper motifs. Wood glue, also called PVA glue (polyvinyl acetate) or white glue, will hold decorative additions securely; also useful for attaching areas of sand and in place of other fillers to bind pigments, clay, and sand applications. All-purpose glue is used to glue things to smaller surfaces; it is waterproof but does not take color well.

Alcohol (methylated spirits): See shellac.

Appliqué: Sewing or gluing decorative additions to a background; examples of suitable materials include glass beads, string, twigs, feathers, seeds, buttons, shells, cut pieces of copper foil, leather, and birch bark (page 195).

Artificial Turpentine or Turpentine Oil: Used to dilute artists' oil paints.

Beads: See appliqué.

Beaten Metal: See gold leaf.

Binders: Mainly synthetic resin binders that are soluble in water and that are used to mix with powdered pigments. Wood glue can also be used as a binder.

Brass Wire: Used like yarn to sew items together, embroider, or wrap decoratively.

Cellulose Lacquer: Used to seal beaten metal that would otherwise oxidize.

Clay: Can be used to create earth colors; used with binders or diluted wood glue (page 190).

Cloths: Used to apply oil colors and paste wax and for polishing; used wet to wipe off partially dried acrylic paint.

Colored Pens: Colored pencils, oils, wax, or pastel chalks for drawing, hatching, or applying designs directly onto the paper or for painting on a background.

Embroidery Floss: For attaching decorative objects such as wooden sticks and cord; the best thread for appliquéing beads (page 195).

Filler: Somewhat grainy, it is applied diluted and mixed with wood glue to give a background a rough texture.

Gold Leaf: Real gold that has been hammered into very thin leaves and is very expensive. A more reasonably priced alternative for gilding is artificial beaten metal or composition gold (page 196).

Knife: Also called a craft knife when it has changeable blades; use wide blades to cut cardboard, narrow blades to cut paper and to carve.

Latex: for the resist technique, can be rubbed off (page 187).

Oil Chalk or Wax Chalk: Used to prevent watery paints from sticking; can also be used for the resist technique (page 189).

Paints: Almost all materials and techniques used in artistic painting, decorative painting, and treatment of wood can be used for paper mache. There are various paints with synthetic resin binders. Among them are acrylic paints, available thick and opaque in tubes or liquid and transparent in bottles. They have many uses for decorating paper mache because they dry waterproof. So–called hobby paints, available in small jars, are synthetic resin paints that dry waterproof. Watercolors—for example, India inks, gouache, pastels, aquarelles, wood stains, and ink—should be sealed with floor wax because they are not waterproof. Oil paints—that is, artists' oil paints—are applied in thin coats and possibly diluted with a few drops of turpentine substitute directly onto white paper or onto a white gesso undercoat (page 184).

Paintbrushes: Wide bristle paintbrushes are used for primers and for painting larger surfaces, in addition to applying paste; narrow ones are used to apply glue and for all work that is hard on a paintbrush (because you scrub more than paint with it). Synthetic hair paintbrushes are suitable for acrylic paints, stains, India inks, and inks, because they are sturdier than natural hair paintbrushes. Marten hair paintbrushes are the best natural hair paintbrushes; they have perfect, elastic tips. Fine work is accomplished much more cleanly and easily than with cheap paintbrushes. Marten hair paintbrushes must be carefully washed with soap and kept in shape by straightening the hairs before drying. Flat hide paintbrushes are good for applications in which you wish to avoid streaks that bristles usually leave.

Paper (for decorative purposes): Use heavy tissue paper for motifs that are to be pasted on, copier paper to make copies of silhouettes, handmade paper for the sandwich technique, and transparent kite paper for mixed color effects (page 192).

Paste Wax: Normally used for polishing floors, it is available as a paste in tubes or as a liquid in canisters. It can be used as a colorless polish that yields a silky sheen for paper mache objects. The solvent it contains can dissolve oil paint that is not yet completely dry. Wait a month before using.

Pastels: Chalk-like crayons used for adding color.

Patina: Available ready to use in bottles; it can also be made from varnish colored lightly with acrylic paint or oil paint. Gesso, heavily diluted with water, can be used for a light patina (page 198).

Pencil: Useful for sketching complicated motifs.

Pigments: These are paints in powdered form. They are available in good craft supply shops and art supply stores. They are mixed with a filler—for example, synthetic resin binder, wood glue, or egg tempera (egg-resin emulsion). Pulverized clay is a natural earth-colored pigment.

Plaster of Paris: Thinned, mixed with wood glue, and applied as a filler.

Primers: Primers contain fillers to even out the background. You can use synthetic resin primers, which are normally used for canvas, or PVA primer, suitable for painting the outside of an object. Gesso is another very useful primer, formerly made from chalk and bone glue, today made of a synthetic resin base and available ready to use from art supply stores (page 184).

Resist Technique: a process in which certain areas of an object are covered with wax, latex, or oil chalk so that paints with a water content will not stick to these areas (page 187).

Sandpaper: Used to sand or polish a background of paper mache and its prime coat of paint or for sanding away layers of paint to create an effect.

Scissors: used to cut out paper motifs (page 193).

Sealants: Acrylic or synthetic resin clear varnish; also paste wax and shellac (page 199).

Shellac: A resin-like secretion of the scale insect; it is available bleached or unbleached in sheets and is dissolved in alcohol; it is also available ready to use in shops (page 199).

Size: Used to attach gold leaf (page 196).

Sponge: Natural sponges are useful for applying irregular dabs of paint.

Stencils: Simple motifs are cut from cardboard or acetate foil, then protected from moisture with varnish. The stencil is held in place while you dab a little paint on the surface with a short, round paintbrush or a cloth.

String: For different types of surface decoration. Package string and cord are pasted or sewn on; thin hemp string can be embroidered on; sisal is good for knots and fringes (page 194).

Toothbrush or Nail Brush: Used for speckling paint. Rub a knife against the bristles so that the paint spatters onto the paper mache object.

Varnishes: see Sealants.

Water Bath: A tin container for heating wax; it often has a handle. In the absence of one of these, a clean tin can will do. The wax is placed in the can, and the can is then placed in a pan filled with water. When the water is simmered slowly and carefully, the wax will melt without getting too hot. *Never heat wax over direct heat; it may catch fire if you do! Never leave heating wax unattended.*

Wax: Ordinary candle wax or batik wax is heated in a container in water for resist techniques and then applied in its liquid state with a paintbrush. The portions covered with wax do not take on color. After the work is done, the wax can be removed by ironing between paper towels or scraping off (page 187).

Index

Suggested Readings

Bawden, Juliet. *The Art and Craft of Paper Mache.* San Francisco: Chronicle Books, 1994.

Jackson, Paul. *The Encyclopedia of Origami and Papercraft Techniques.* Philadelphia: Running Press, 1991.

Shannon, Faith. *The Art and Craft of Paper.* San Francisco: Chronicle Books, 1994.